TRANSACTIONS

of the

American Philosophical Society

Held at Philadelphia for Promoting Useful Knowledge

VOLUME 77, Part 5, 1987

Dante and the Book of the Cosmos

JOHN G. DEMARAY

THE AMERICAN PHILOSOPHICAL SOCIETY

Independence Square, Philadelphia

1987

This publication was subsidized in part
by the Jayne Fund.

Library of Congress Catalog
Card Number 86-72887
International Standard Book Number 0-87169-775-0
US ISSN 0065-9746

"La mente tua conservi quel ch'udito
  hai contra te," mi comandò quel saggio;
    "e ora attendi qui," e drizzò 'l dito:
"quando sarai dinanzi al dolce raggio
  di quella, il cui bell' occhio tutto vede,
    da lei saprai di tua vita il vïaggio."

Virgil's words to Dante in
the city of Dis
(*Inf.* X, 127–133)

"Let your memory recall what you have heard
  against you," the Sage declared to me; "and
    now mark here," and he raised his finger:
"when you shall stand before the sweet ray of
  that Lady, whose bright eyes see all, from her
    you shall know the journey of your life."

CONTENTS

LIST OF ILLUSTRATIONS

ACKNOWLEDGMENTS

Grateful acknowledgment is made of a Huntington Library Resident Fellowship and a National Endowment for the Humanities Research Grant in support of this section of an extended work-in-progress—researched in Great Britain, Europe, and Israel—on *mimesis* in Renaissance literature. I am indebted to the Rutgers University Research Council for an award that facilitated the completion of this present book, and to the New York Public Library for access to a rich research collection and for use of the Frederick Lewis Allen Room. Appreciated also is assistance from individual staff members of the Bibliothèque Nationale; British Library; Princeton University Library; Royal Geographical Society Library, London; and the Bibliotèca Vaticana.

My special gratitude is expressed to Painton Cowen for permission to reproduce photographs in his *Rose Windows* published by Thames and Hudson.

Warm thanks for advice or academic assistance are due William Anderson, Norman Burns, Horton Davies, Joan Ferrante, S. K. Heninger, John Lyerle, Frederick Main, Elizabeth McLachman, John M. Steadman, James Thorpe, William Ringler, Marcel Thiebeaux, and Fr. Dunstan Tucker. I am obligated to pilgrim text editors Fr. Bellarmino Bagatti and Fr. Sabino de Sandoli for generous help at the Franciscan Library, Jerusalem. Julia Bolton Holloway and Joseph Tusiani are owed particular thanks for incisive criticism of a draft of the Dante chapter; and Carole Le Faivre, for excellent editorial suggestions. Any inadequacies in the completed study are entirely those of the author. As always, I am most deeply indebted for encouragement, advice, and scholarly criticism to Hannah Disinger Demaray who—having read from the Bible and early literature while journeying over full chains of pilgrimage "stations" in the Holy Land, Europe, and England—knows as few others the meaning and form of the medieval Book of the World.

I. ARCHITECTURAL TYPOLOGY AND STRUCTURE IN THE *COMMEDIA*

Two fervent spiritual desires underlie Dante's figural pilgrimage to Beatrice at the end of the *Vita Nuova* and in the *Commedia:* a passionate longing of love to overcome error and sin in this life by finding as a pilgrim the true pathways to the holiest temples in the holiest cities associated with this lady; and at the same time, an overwhelming yearning of love to transcend this mortal realm of suffering and death, to rise through spiritual pilgrimage to a vision of Beatrice in heaven. Such desires of intellect and will, giving force to the rational conviction that pilgrimage on earth is a prefiguration of spiritual ascent in the world beyond, serve as a basis for the structure of Dante's *Commedia* and, when considered apart from Beatrice, of elements in contemporaneous medieval religious architecture. In its encyclopedic scope and its relation of earth to heaven, the poem is an analogue for pilgrimage "temples" and churches that in the late Middle Ages were widely considered architectural representations of the external physical and immaterial universe.[1]

---

[1] George Duby in *The Age of the Cathedrals, Art and Society, 980–1420,* trans. Eleanor Levieux and Barbara Thompson (Chicago, 1981), analyzes the cathedrals as types for the cosmos and the city of heaven, and discusses parallel elements in the "cosmic" philosophical–theological views of Abbot Suger, builder of St. Denis in Paris, and of St. Bernard, Abbot of Clairvaux and Dante's last guide in the *Commedia.* Duby, placing primary emphasis upon French structures, concludes his study of cathedral building projects of the 1250–1280 period by remarking that the "*Divine Comedy* may be regarded as a cathedral, the last." Calling attention to one of several clerical teaching orders in Dante's home city, Duby suggests that the poet "based the *Commedia* on what he had learned of scholastic theology from the Dominican preachers of Florence who had studied at the university of Paris. Like the great cathedrals of France, this poem leads in successive stages, according to the enlightened hierarchies of Dionysius the Areopagite and through the intercession of Saint Bernard . . . and the Virgin, to the love that moves the stars. As a poetics of the incarnation, the art of the great cathedrals had wonderfully celebrated the body of Christ, in other words, . . . the world itself" (p. 187).

In *The Gothic Cathedral: Origins of Gothic Architecture and the Medieval Concept of Order* (Princeton, 1956), Otto von Simson reveals how the cosmic typology of the medieval cathedral, like that of Dante's *Commedia,* is based upon an imitation of the Work of God realized in the created universe, and the Word of God realized in the Incarnation. He writes that the "cathedral was the intimation of ineffable truth. The medieval cosmos was theologically transparent. The Creation appeared as the first of God's revelations, the Incarnation of the Word as the second. Between these two theophanies medieval man perceived innumerable mystical correspondences, and only he who understood these correspondences understood the ultimate meaning and structure of the cosmos." The divine order of the cosmos, corrupted on the earthly plane by Adam's fall, was still dominantly "manifest in the harmony of the heavenly spheres." This divine order, von Simson finds, was in turn reflected in the work of both Dante and the cathedral builders, medieval artists who sought to reproduce the structure of the cosmos. He notes that the cathedral in its symbolism is "at once a 'model' of the cosmos and

1

The medieval conception of the universe as a figural model for religious buildings arose from many early sources, among them St. Augustine's discussion of the order of the cosmos in *De ordine* 2:39, and the remarks of Macrobius in *Commentarius ex Cicerone in somnium Scipionis* 1:14, on that order in which he describes the universe as a "cosmic temple." Medieval builders of religious edifices were also clearly inspired by passages in the Book of Revelation 21:2–31, describing the descending heavenly city, the New Jerusalem, resplendent in "pure gold, like to transparent glass." Influential too were passages in Proverbs 8:27, and Ezekiel 40:3, that were interpreted as alluding to divine architectural creation. Numerological proportions in medieval religious edifices were developed—though the exact degree of influence has been questioned and debated—using cosmic proportions cited in Plato's *Timaeus* and supposedly advanced also by Pythagoras, and by referring to biblical passages on the size of Solomon's Temple.

The *Commedia*, it should be recalled, depicts a pilgrimage in this life and beyond in the Easter Season of 1300, a period when, according to Giovanni Villani in his *Croniche Fiorentine*, two hundred thousand pilgrims thronged to temples and basilicas in Rome during the Church's first Jubilee Pilgrimage. Villani states that it was his own participation in the important event of this pilgrimage—together with his reading of Virgil, Sallust, Paulus Orosius and other "masters of history" who recorded important events of times past—that inspired him to write his chronicle.[2] The first page of a contemporaneous manuscript commentary on the *Commedia*, produced in Pisa in 1335, in fact contains a drawing of pilgrims bowed before Boniface

---

an image of the Celestial City. If the architect designed his sanctuary according to the laws of harmonious proportion, he not only imitated the order of the visible world, but conveyed an intimation, inasmuch as that is possible to man, of the perfection of the world to come" (pp. 35–37). Commenting upon the "archetypes of the Christian sanctuary" that "actually inspired the medieval builder," von Simson makes the now well recognized point that in general the figural structure of the medieval "church was conceived as an image of the Celestial Jerusalem, but . . . the Celestial Jerusalem in turn was thought to have been prefigured in the Solomonic Temple" (p. 11).

Other recent discussions of the medieval cathedral as a type of the cosmos include those by Charles Terrasse, in his chapters "Le miroir de la nature" and "Le miroir historique" in *La cathédrale: miroir du monde*, rev. ed. (Paris, 1954), 72–89, 112–114; William Anderson and Clive Hicks, *Cathedrals in Britain and Ireland from early times to the reign of Henry VIII* (New York, 1978), 13–19; Wim Swaan, *The Gothic Cathedral*, intro. Christopher Brooke (New York, 1969), 48–56; and William Alexander McClung, *The Architecture of Paradise: Survivals of Eden and Jerusalem* (Berkeley, Los Angeles, and London, 1983), 69–75.

In *L'Italia nella Divina Commedia* (Milano, 1923), Paolo Revelli, citing specific T-and-O world maps and other early geographic-iconographic materials, offers authoritative insights into Dante's medieval iconographic view of the world; see in particular the chapters "Le terre che Dante vide" (pp. 1–13); "La cultura geografica di Dante" (pp. 3–27); and "Dante e le carte del suo tempo" (pp. 31–40). Excellent examples of medieval T-and-O maps of the thirteenth and fourteenth centuries—maps showing Egypt, Mt. Sinai, and Jerusalem—can be found in *Monumenta Cartographica Vaticana*, 2 vols. (Città del Vaticano, 1944).

[2] *Croniche Fiorentine*, trans. Rose E. Selfe, Philip H. Wicksteed, ed. (London, 1906), Bk. 8, sec. 36, pp. 320–321. See too *Inf.* XVIII, 28–33, for Dante's well-known and presumably eyewitness reference to pilgrims in the Jubilee Year of 1300 crossing the bridge of Castel St. Angelo before St. Peter's Basilica.

VIII, the pope who granted exceptional Jubilee indulgences in 1300 to pilgrims visiting the holiest basilicas of the eternal city.[3]

Like the processional architecture of these and other Byzantine-Romanesque basilicas of the fourth through the eleventh centuries, and of numerous Italian and northern European reconstructions of the round "temple" of the Holy Sepulchre largely of the eleventh century and later, Dante's processional poem contains representations of pilgrimage "stations" and holy "centers" in the medieval iconographic Book of the earth or world, representations through which the pilgrim passes re-enacting and fulfilling in his own spiritual life past biblical events that occurred far away at the signified holy sites. And like Tuscan and French Gothic processional cathedrals of the twelfth century and later with their comprehensive pilgrimage elements, Dante's poem is constructed to depict a pilgrim's fulfilling movement, not only past stations in this world, but also within the larger Book of the Cosmos comprising the spheres and the Empyrean. In cathedrals it was the arrangement of iconographic "types" or *figurae* that made such processional movement possible. Designs in nave floors and associated icons often signified the pilgrim's pathway to Jerusalem; altars through their iconography represented the holy "temple altars" in that city; and the great wheel-rose windows above, flooded with heavenly light illuminating the ordered icons of the elect, pointed to the Church Triumphant in heaven.

Medieval biblical "typology" or "figurism" was, of course, thought to provide one means by which artists and others could apprehend and depict the "true" structure of external reality and universal history. The "true" words of scripture, Church Fathers such as Origen and Augustine and Gregory of Nyssa averred, could in their literal sense do no other than objectively signify true epochal events—events considered as "types" or *figurae* and represented by artists in appropriate verbal or visual forms— involving "historical" persons, places, and things. Applying what came to be known as the "allegory of the theologians" to biblical texts, the Church Fathers, as is well known, bound together Old and New Testament history by indicating how in the chain of universal Hebraic-Christian history each epochal event, the type or *figura*, foreshadowed and then was fulfilled in the next, the anti-type. Thus the epochal event of the Exodus, the type, was seen to prefigure the epochal event of the Redemption, the anti-type. The Redemption then became the type or *figura* that was next observed to foreshadow the Transfiguration, the anti-type, and so on to the end of the world and the eternal bliss of souls in heaven. Abstract or "mystical" meanings could only arise from what was considered the incontestable fact of scripture's literal historical sense.

---

[3] A reproduction of the illustration appears in Peter Preiger, Millard Meiss, and Charles S. Singleton, *Illuminated Manuscripts of the Divine Comedy* (Princeton, 1969), vol. 2; plate 6b of Chantilly Musée Condé ms. 579, fol. 33.

Just as "historical" figural or typological events were thought to be in-dicated by the language of the Book of God's Words, the Bible, so too were these same "historical" events believed to be signified by iconographic markings—visual "types" in the form of relics, stones, rivers, mountains, and other landmarks, and heavenly bodies—in the corresponding Book of God's Works, the created world and cosmos. The patterned "historical" iconography pointed to by the "words" and markings of these absolutely "true" divine source books was then replicated by artists and builders in the iconographic *figurae* of paintings, mosaics, sculpture, stained glass win-dows, cosmographical illustrations, church architecture, and literature. The churches and other works were designed in part to motivate persons to comprehend and to re-enact the depicted episodes, through spiritual med-itation and ritualistic action, and thus to fulfill in their own lives the spiritual pattern and meaning of true divine history.

Architectural-literary figural criticism of the *Commedia* has in general concentrated upon comparisons of individual "architectural" elements in Dante's poem and in medieval churches, exposing, for example, how the iconographic "types" in earthly wheel-rose windows, such as the one in the basilica of San Zeno, Verona, are fulfilled in Dante's transcendent rose of heaven.[4] Yet the sheer volume of iconographic subject matter, together with the difficulty in establishing an embracing critical perspective, has to a large degree limited comparisons of over-all typology to an analysis of Gothic elements of number, structure, multiplicity, and unifying types.[5] The influence upon Dante of that very popular medieval architectural form, the Byzantine "temple" round church, has been neglected, as has the in-fluence of Byzantine architectural figurism in general.[6]

Recently the medieval Book of God's Words, the Bible, and the medieval Book of the World, with Jerusalem at the supposed center of the northern hemisphere's land-mass, have been examined in detail and related to the figural structure of the *Commedia*. Dante's journey beyond life in the Jubilee Pilgrimage year of 1300 has been interpreted as a fulfillment of corre-

---

[4] John Leyerle includes an interpretation, diagrams and photographs of the San Zeno wheel-rose window in "The Rose-Wheel Design and Dante's *Paradiso*," *University of Toronto Quarterly* 40, number 3 (Spring, 1977): 280–307. See also Giuseppe C. Di Scipio's comments on what are regarded as octagonal elements in Dante's rose and cathedral wheel-rose windows in "The Symbolic Rose in Dante's *Paradiso*," and especially the chapter "The Rose and the Gothic Cathedral" (pp. 150–177), City University of New York Doctoral Dissertation, 1977. Di Scipio, without mentioning rose-wheel windows, offers a symbolic reading of Dante's rose in "The Structure of the Rose in Dante's *Paradiso*," *Canadian Journal of Italian Studies* 2, no. 1–2 (Fall–Winter, 1978–1979): 19–39.

[5] For example, see Erwin Panofsky, *Gothic Architecture and Scholasticism* (Latrobe, 1951); and H. O. Taylor, *The Classical Heritage of the Middle Ages*, rev. ed. (New York, 1911), 315ff. See also the comparative, analogical structural analysis of Dante's *Vita Nuova* and figural elements in Gothic cathedrals in Jerome Mazzaro's *The Figure of Dante: An Essay on the Vita Nuova* (Princeton, 1981), 51–70.

[6] Giovanni Fallani in *Dante e la cultura figurativa medievale* (Milano, Firenze, Roma, and other cities, 1971) shows the influence of a great range of medieval art works upon Dante, including the Byzantine, but without associating the works specifically to architectural figurism.

sponding events foreshadowed both in biblical history and in a great circle long pilgrimage over "stations" leading from worldly Egypt, to holy Jerusalem, and then to eternal Rome.[7] The biblical-pilgrimage typology of

---

[7] For citations to the voluminous body of pilgrim texts, together with readings of great circle Egypt-Jerusalem-Rome pilgrimage typology in the *Vita Nuova* and the *Commedia*, see John G. Demaray's "Patterns of Earthly Pilgrimage in Dante's *Commedia*: Palmers, Romers, and the Great Circle Journey," *Romance Philology* (Nov., 1970): 239–258; and *The Invention of Dante's Commedia* (New Haven and London, 1974). The especially famed pilgrimage practices on the Jerusalem "ring" of Redemption stations, involving through the centuries the greatest number of Latin pilgrims and crusaders to the Near East, are figured in varying ways both in Dante's Eden and in later Roman Catholic stations-of-the-Cross ritual. Practices on the remote stations of the Exodus, involving fewer persons, were generally lost to Catholic ritual but are apparent in figured actions on the slopes of Dante's Mt. Purgatory. The "Transfiguring" stations of Rome, figured at the end of Dante's *Paradiso*, entered formally into Catholic Jubilee Year ritual, of course, with Boniface VIII's proclamation of the Jubilee pilgrimage of 1300. Dante's wide knowledge of Holy Land pilgrimage sites has been documented by a former Franciscan Custodian of the Holy Land, Fr. P. Ferdinando Diotallevi, in the inclusive *Dante ed i luoghi santi* (Jerusalem, 1921). Fr. Diotallevi draws attention to a range of references in the *Commedia* to medieval Holy Land pilgrimage stations, but he does not develop a structured interpretation of the poem.

In reading the *Commedia* as an allegory of the theologians, William Anderson in *Dante the Maker* (London and Boston, 1980), relates the great circle Egypt-Jerusalem-Rome pilgrimage typology of the poem's literal sense to the spiritual senses of allegory particularly as reflected in the steps of traditional meditative literature. Anderson, striking a welcome critical balance in discussing Dante's medieval conflation of the physical and the immaterial, reveals how spiritual and visionary meanings are joined in the *Commedia* with an "historical," figural imitation of worldly and biblical events. Anderson discloses that through the art of the *Commedia* Dante, in making the opening stage of his pilgrimage beyond life to Beatrice in an Earthly Paradise located at the antipodes of the southern hemisphere opposite Jerusalem in the northern hemisphere, "recapitulates and transfers to another plane where they can be satisfied the longings of generations of Crusaders and pilgrims for the true Jerusalem." Elaborating upon the identification of Dante's Eden as a fulfilled antitype of the earthly Jerusalem, and of the poet's heavenly city of the rose as the fulfilled antitype of Rome, Anderson maintains that "just as Jerusalem is a stage on the Great Circle pilgrimage for reaching the final goal of Rome, so Beatrice points to the civilization that will appear with the world emperor and the Christianization of the themes of antiquity" (pp. 372–373).

Peter Armour in *The Door of Purgatory: A Study of Multiple Symbolism in Dante's Purgatorio* (Oxford, 1983) has recently argued that the "special religious and redemptive significance" of the Jubilee year of 1300 pilgrimage to Rome accounts for the central symbolism of the *Commedia* (p. 154). In this symbolic reading that leans heavily upon empirical facts about Dante's life, Armour accepts that Dante's movement to the rose in *Paradiso* reflects an earthly Romer's pilgrimage to the eternal city; but by placing what seems to me too much weight upon empirical biographical evidence at the expense of medieval figural relations, he takes issue with the view that the poet's journey beyond in *Purgatorio* is the fulfillment in the literal sense of a foreshadowing terrestrial pilgrimage from Egypt to Jerusalem. "The main difficulty in this theory," he writes, "is, of course, that, whilst there is some evidence that Dante made a pilgrimage from Florence to Rome, there is none at all that he ever made one to the Holy Land" (p. 160). Armour, however, incorporates the symbolic meaning of the full great circle journey into his interpretation of Dante's pilgrimage to the heavenly rose: "Under one aspect, his journey is an exodus and pilgrimage of a living man from the Egypt of this world to a Holy Land and the new Jerusalem (*Par.* XXV, 55–56). Perhaps it is that pilgrimage which, because of Boniface's indifference, Dante was unable to make in his real life (cf. *Par.* IX, 126, 136–38). Under another aspect, it is also a transformation of a pilgrimage which he almost certainly did make to Rome, and so he chose to express the personal and the universal redemptive significance of the poem, setting it also in the Jubilee year" (p. 159). For a typological analysis that differs from this modern empirical view of what constitutes Dante's "real" past life and earthly pilgrimage, see footnote 44.

World and poem, however, can be further illumined through comparison with the parallel typology of medieval churches and "temples" of Byzantine and Romanesque as well as Gothic design. In particular, close examination is still required of Dante's integrating "cosmic" light and wheel icons—among them, the circles in the stars referred to by the poet as an "angelico templo" (*Par.* XXVIII, 53), and the circular court of heaven called "nostra basilica" by Beatrice (*Par.* XXV, 30)—as they relate to wider church and temple iconography and to the figural structure of *Purgatorio* and *Paradiso*.[8] These circular icons, derived in part from earthly round church, basilica, and cathedral architecture, are types that have their ultimate fulfillment in an all-containing "volume": the Book of the entire "Cosmos" viewed by Dante during the Beatific Vision (*Par.* XXXIII, 86).

The Book of the created universe is dramatically revealed to the poet in the Empyrean when he looks upon what, to his finite human faculties, appears as "the universal form of this knot" (*Par.* XXXIII, 91: "La forma universal di questo nodo"): the simple flame, or "semplice lume," that unites in a single volume, bound together by love and ingathered in Godhead, all the leaves of the universe:

> Nel suo profondo vidi che s'interna,
>   legato con amore in un volume,
>   ciò che per l'universo si squaderna;
> sustanze e accidenti e lor costume,
>   quasi conflati insieme. . . .
>
> (Par. XXXIII, 85–89)

> Within its depths I saw ingathered, bound by
>   love in one volume, the scattered leaves
>   of all the universe;
> Substance and accidents and their relations,
>   as though together fused. . . .

"S'interna" can possibly be associated with "terno" or trinity which holds together, as commentary has suggested, the pages of the cosmic book with the number three of spirit.[9] The words "si squaderna," meaning scattered or unbound, imply "quaderni" or "four each," and so connote the number four of matter, the physical substance of the universe. "Si squaderna" also connotes the four sheets of parchment, the "quaderno" or quire of medieval manuscripts, which were folded and cut to make eight leaves of a book.

---

[8] The text of the *Commedia* used throughout is Dante Alighieri, *La Divina Commedia secondo l'antica vulgata*, ed. Giorgio Petrocchi, 4 vols. (Milano, A. Mondadori for the Società Dantesca Italiana, 1965–69) and reprinted in the edition of C. H. Grandgent, rev. Charles S. Singleton (Cambridge, Mass., 1972).

[9] See Charles S. Singleton's notes for *The Divine Comedy: Paradiso, 2. Commentary* (Princeton, 1975), 576–578.

The simple flame that is the "forma universal" then transfigures, because of the increasing power of Dante's vision, into one paradoxical simple semblance, or "simplice sembiante," that appears as three rotating circles or "giri" of light that finally reflect within themselves our human image or "nostra effige" (*Par.* XXXIII, 109–131).

Dante's poetic narrative will be seen ultimately to derive from the transcendent, subsuming Book of the Cosmos ingathered in Godhead. Concurrently, Dante's narrative will also be seen to derive from figural centers of journey, associated with biblical history, in this physical world. By ingeniously inverting and yet preserving figural bonds joining earthly and heavenly types, the poet makes those types in *Paradiso* refer most directly to the transcendent light and wheel icons signifying God; and those in the *Inferno* and *Purgatorio* refer to this transcendent center but also to figured centers on earth.[10]

The icons of Godhead sustain, fulfill, and synthesize the antithetical or complementary earthly centers: the central interior "tomba" of Satan within the physical globe (*Inf.* XXXIV, 128); the tomb and cross of Christ, the second Adam, in a Jerusalem temple at the center of the northern hemisphere (*Inf.* XXXIV, 1–3, 112–117); the nest or "nido" of the human race and the traditional tomb of the first Adam in Eden at the center of the southern hemisphere (*Purg.* XXVIII, 78; XXXII, 37); and the tomb and temple of St. Peter, the Father of the Church, in an earthly eternal city that is a type for the heavenly city in which the saint appears enthroned on high (*Par.* XXVII, 22–27; XXXII, 124–130).[11]

Satan in falling to his "tomba" within the earth, Virgil explains in *Inferno* XXXIV, caused the land of the southern hemisphere to flee; this land then gathered in the northern hemisphere with the temple and tomb of Christ at the geographic center (*Inf.* XXXIV, 124–129). Dante, in turning from the northern to the southern hemisphere on the hairy sides of Satan, is informed by Virgil that, though in hell, he is under Jerusalem where Christ was "consuto," obviously "consumed" through Redemption on the cross (114).

The iconographic-figural relationship between the Jerusalem and Rome temples is illustrated by St. Peter's words among the stars. St. Peter, in fact emphasizing the true sanctity of his temple and tomb in Rome by denouncing their desecration under Pope Boniface VIII, echoes the phraseology and words of Jeremiah (7:4) who had three times used the term "temple" in crying out against the despoiling of the holy Jerusalem Temple

---

[10] For comments on Dante's Beatific Vision in *Paradiso* as the "inceptive cause" of the *Commedia*, see Helen Dunbar, *Symbolism in Medieval Thought* (New York, 1961), 29–30; Anderson, *Dante the Maker*, 335–337; Erich Auerbach, *Dante: Poet of the Secular World*, trans. Ralph Manheim (Chicago, 1961), 94; and Demaray, *The Invention of Dante's Commedia*, 59–63.

[11] As John Freccero has shown in "The Sign of Satan," *Modern Language Notes* 80 (1965): 11–26, Satan with his six grotesque wings in the "tomba" of the pit of hell is an anti-type for the Redeeming Christ on the cross in Jerusalem.

of the Lord. Peter decries Boniface who, the saint insists, "usurps upon earth my place, my place, my place" (*Par.* XXVII, 22: "usurpa in terra il luoco mio,/il luoco mio, il luoco mio"). Peter then states that Boniface "has made my burial ground a sewer for blood and stench, whereby the apostate one who fell from here above, is soothed down there below" (*Par.* XXVII, 25–27: "fatto ha del cimitero mio cloaca/ del sangue e della puzza, onde il perverso,/ che cadde di quassu, laggiu si placa").

At the "temple" site of Christ's tomb and cross at the Christian geographic "center" of Jerusalem, anonymous pilgrims of the twelfth and later centuries recorded, a conduit in the rock of Golgotha allowed Christ's blood to flow upon the supposed skull of Adam in the cave beneath (fn. 46). And in the *Commedia* at the old prefiguring pagan world geographic center of Crete, where a chaste pagan king is said to have once ruled over the world, the idol of an Old Man signifying humanity is entombed within Mt. Ida. With eyes turned toward Rome and shoulders toward Egyptian Damietta, the idol weeps red rivulets that flow down to the lake of Cocytus which entombs Satan (*Inf.* XIV, 94–120). Now in Rome at the temple and tomb of St. Peter, the Apostolic successor of Christ, a sewer rather than a conduit exists through which blood and stench passes and so soothes Satan in the pit of hell.

Dante, in creating and locating his earthly tomb and temple figurism to accommodate the assumed spiritual iconographic order of this physical world, thus becomes the consummate exponent in poetry of an actual medieval architectural mode studied at length by André Grabar: the figural Martyrium temple-tomb marking a spiritual-geographic center and related through earthly types and anti-types to the tomb of Christ in Jerusalem.[12]

---

[12] Grabar in his comprehensive *Martyrium: Recherches sur le culte des reliques et l'art Chrétien antique,* 3 vols. (Paris, 1943–1946) provides an analysis of how religious edifices such as Old St. Peter's; St. Paul's; the Lateran; St. Vitale, Ravenna; San Stefano, Bologna; and other European structures were designed to a significant degree as figural reflections of the round Church of the Holy Sepulchre or Byzantine basilica Martyria in the Near East. Martyria in Rome and elsewhere in the West, Grabar shows, were constructed over the relics of saints and holy persons and used as pilgrim shrines. In disclosing the Near Eastern Byzantine influence on the typological form of European medieval religious edifices, Grabar, in volume one (1946) includes actual or projected ground plans of the fourth-century Church of the Holy Sepulchre (fig. 37); the Church of the Nativity, Bethlehem (fig. 27); Old St. Peter's, Rome, with its two southern circular Martyria (fig. 22); Old Maria Maggiore, Rome (fig. 46); the crypt of St. Apollinare, Ravenna (fig. 118); medieval plans for circular Martyrium structures by Fra Giocondo, Florence (fig. 74); and the old Abbey of St. Augustine with its round Martyrium, Canterbury, about A.D. 1050 (fig. 91). Photographs are contained in volume three (1946) of fifth-century Byzantine mosaics, in the apse of St. Pudenziana in Rome, of pilgrimage sites in Jerusalem (pl. 39); and of a number of Byzantine Transfiguration mosaics of similar design in the Church of the Transfiguration, St. Catherine's Monastery, Mt. Sinai; in St. Apollinare, Ravenna (pl. 41); in St. Vitale, Ravenna; and in SS. Cosma and Damiano, Rome (pl. 42). See also Jean Paul Richter, *Die mosaiken von Ravenna* (Wien, 1878), pp. 103–104, for an early comparison of the Transfiguration mosaics at St. Apollinare and the Church of the Transfiguration, Mt. Sinai.

Numerous medieval bottles and amulets, excavated in the small northern Italian town of Bobbio and showing images of the cupola of Christ's Jerusalem tomb and other Holy Land pilgrimage sites, are examined by André Grabar in *Ampoules de Terre Sainte* (Paris, 1958). See also Grabar's *I'iconoclasme byzantine; dossier archeologique* (Paris, 1957).

THE WORLD BOOK AND CORRESPONDING TYPES:
NATURE AND ART

An analysis of Dante's culminating temple and circle icons requires preparation. To gain perspective on what may at first seem the bewildering diversity and multiplicity of medieval pilgrimage typology, preliminary but still rather extended suggestions have to be made on a complex subject: how corresponding typological structures can be discerned in the iconographic Book of the World, the Bible, medieval churches, and Dante's *Commedia*. A unifying point of view is indeed possible. While medieval pilgrimage typology is nominalist in its encyclopedic multiplication of individual types, it is mystical in its attempts to absorb and harmonize this multiplicity in patterned structures of synthesizing anti-types which eventually are represented as merging in the oneness of Infinite Being. The corresponding structures of anti-types in the World, the Bible, churches, and Dante's poem come into focus when types are examined, not in "static" and sometimes confusing one-to-one comparisons, but in terms of their

---

Richard Krautheimer in an important study examines figural architectural reproductions of the Rotunda or Anastasis of the Holy Sepulchre in "Introduction to an 'Iconography of Medieval Architecture,'" first published in the *Journal of the Warburg and Courtault Institutes* 5 (1942): 1–33, and reprinted with a postscript and additional bibliography in Krautheimer's *Studies in Early Christian, Medieval, and Renaissance Art* (New York and London, 1969), 115–150. Krautheimer argues that even the "Baptistery of S. Giovanni at Florence" and other baptisteries, though having forms derived in part from those of ancient mausolea, at times "went further and actually copied the model of the Anastasis in Jerusalem, where Christ had risen from His tomb, setting the prototype of resurrection and symbolically of baptism" (pp. 138–139). And Ernest Hatch Wilkins, without referring to the wider literature and iconography of the Latin-Byzantine pilgrimage tradition, maintains in "Dante and the Mosaics of his 'Bel San Giovanni,'" *Speculum* 2 (1927): 1–10, reprinted in *Dante In America: the First Two Centuries*, ed. A. Bartlett Giamatti (Binghamton, 1983), 144–159, that the thirteenth-century, Byzantine-style mosaics on the lower band of the S. Giovanni Baptistery copula influenced the depiction in *Purgatorio* XXVII of Dante's entry into the Earthly Paradise, the other-worldly realm that has been found to contain actual antitypes for the "Temple" of the Holy Sepulchre in Jerusalem (See note 41). Giovanni Fallani, concentrating in detail upon edifices and art works in medieval Italy, has called attention in *Dante e la cultura figurative medievale*, 99–100, to iconographic similarities in the processional Byzantine mosaics of St. Apollinare, Ravenna; and St. Paul's, Rome; and in the figural representation of Beatrice's processional appearance with her train in the Earthly Paradise.

European and English figural imitations of the Church of the Holy Sepulchre and other Jerusalem edifices are discussed by Alfred W. Chaplan, *St. John of Jerusalem, Clerkenwell* (London, 1922), 38–42; and by Elizabeth Wheeler Schermerhorn, *On the Trail of the Eight-Pointed Cross: A Study of the Heritage of the Knights Hospitallers in Feudal Europe* (New York, 1940), 300–305. English round churches as types of the Holy Sepulchre are examined by William St. John Hope, "Round Naved Churches of England," *Report of the Chapter General for the Year 1916* (London, 1916) in a contemporary British Hospitallers Association publication; Henry W. Fincham, "The Priory Church of St. John at Clerkenwell," *The Journal of the British Archeological Association* (December, 1911): 183–189; Charles Lucas, "Eglises Circulaires," *Des Annales de la Société Central des Architectes* 12, first series (1881): 39–64.

Despite the pervasiveness of processional pilgrimage world figurism in round churches, basilicas, and cathedrals, much of the earthly typology of the edifices, like the related figurism of early processional liturgy and of corresponding internalized "steps" taken in meditation, still requires study in the full light of the massive great circle pilgrimage literature and iconography on the "stations" of the Exodus and on the "rings" of steps or "stations" at Mt. Sinai, Jerusalem, and Rome.

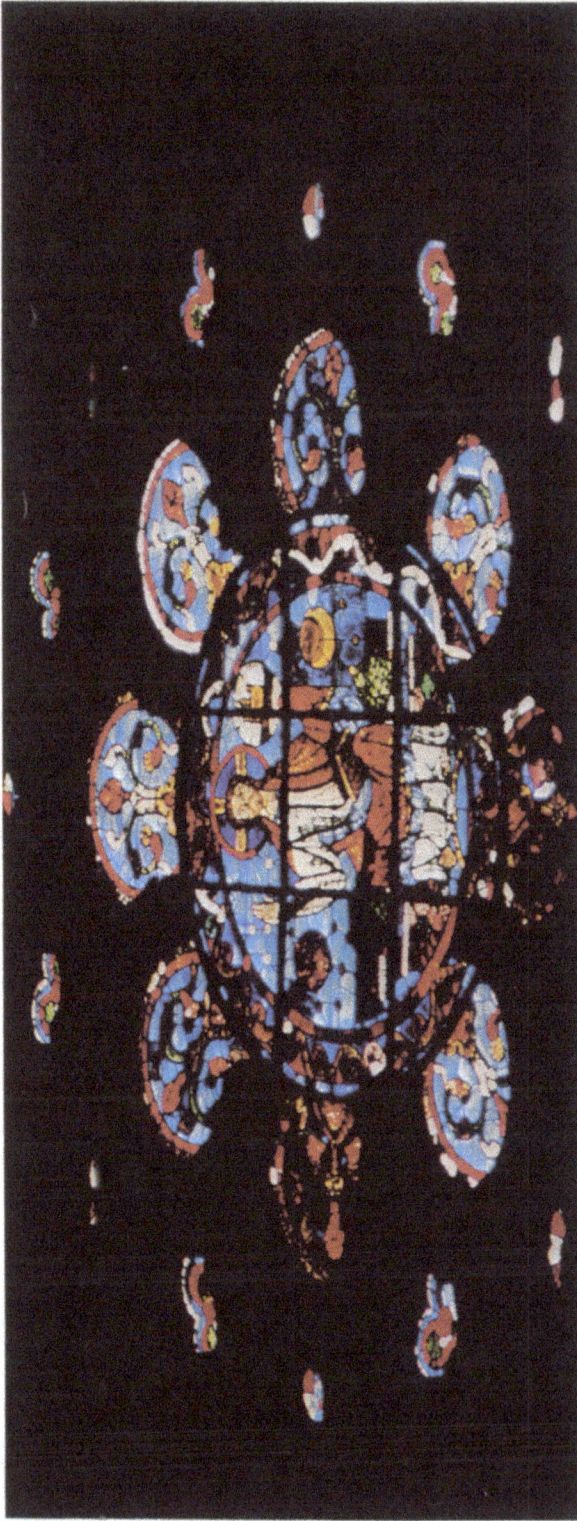

FIG. 1. The two ultimate medieval source books of "historical" figurism and structure of the *Commedia*, are depicted in this mid-thirteenth century rosette window, Chartres.

Christ as the Logos, with right hand raised in blessing, sits enthroned at the center of the cosmos, the circular earthly world upheld in his left hand over the Bible on his left knee. At the center of the world held by Christ, a spired building appears in the position traditionally used to signify Jerusalem and its temples. Around Christ in the main window are the bodies of the material heavens: the sun on His right, the moon on His left; six enveloping planets colored red; and enveloping white and yellow stars.

sequential, progressively unfolding operation and effect upon the acting reader, worshipper, or pilgrim.

In his famous lecture on the desire of the human intellect and will to move toward true objects of love, Virgil in *Purgatorio* XVIII, citing the substantial forms of objects, carefully explains in philosophic terminology this medieval "operational principle" of progressive perception and apprehension.

> Ogne forma sustanzïal, che setta
>   è da materia ed è con lei unita
>   specifica virtute ha in sé colletta,
> la qual sanza operar non è sentita,
>   né si dimostra mai che per effetto,
>   come per verdi fronde in pianta vita.
> Però là onde vegna lo 'ntelletto
>   de le prime notizie, omo non sape
>
> (49–56)

> Every substantial form, which is distinct from
>   matter and is in union with it, has a specific
>   virtue contained within itself
> which is not perceived save in operation, nor is
>   manifested except by its effects, just as life
>   in a plant by the green leaves.
> Therefore man knows not whence the understanding
>   of the first cognitions may come

Knowledge of medieval types was similarly gained through their operation and effect, even though the sources of certain "first cognitions" were incomprehensible. In the World, the Bible, churches, and Dante's poem, unifying types were arranged, or were conceived as being arranged, progressively to enlighten the reader-actor engaged in external processional and interior meditative activity. Thirteenth and fourteenth-century religious humanism placed stress upon each person's acting out the journey of this life, the journey of decision on earth that foreshadowed the person's fulfilled eternal destiny. When viewed from the perspective of the moving reader-actor, the multiple elements of pilgrimage typology become ever more coherent and can be observed to guide the reader-actor in a spiritual ascent from "station" to "station," and from associated meditative step to step, toward hoped-for union with God.

This processional outlook is essential to a critical appreciation of the range of pilgrimage typology. By placing recent architectural criticism of medieval churches in the perspective of medieval processional pilgrimage literature; by making processional on-site inspections of "stations" and churches on the Egypt-Jerusalem-Rome route and in Europe; and then by using pilgrimage typology to gain insight into the unfolding typology of the *Commedia*, all-embracing figural patterns in the World, the Bible,

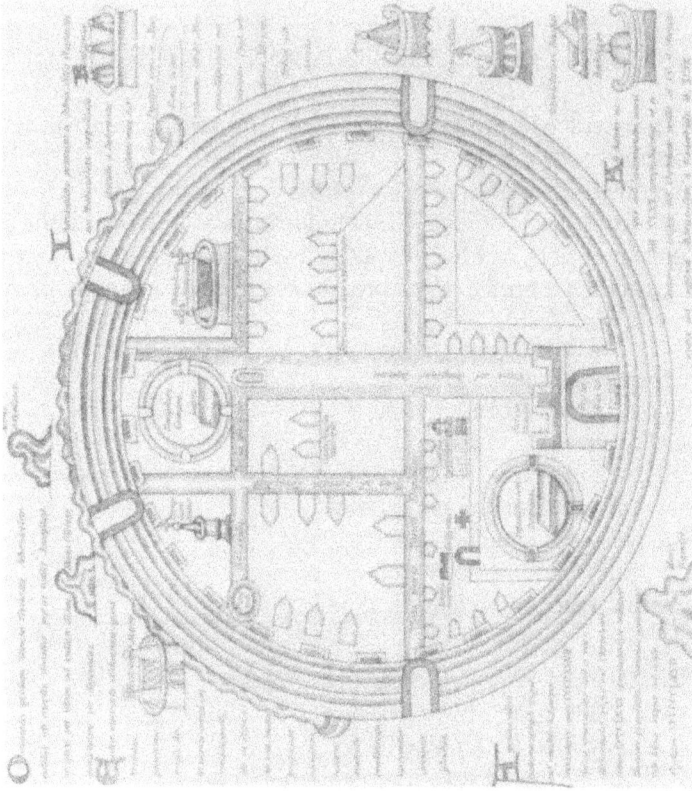

Fig. 3. "Stations" of the Redemption near the Holy Sepulchre's circular Anastasis, divided here with T-and-O type zonal lines, are depicted in this crusader map of Jerusalem (ca. 1160) from *Itinera Hierosolymitana Crucesignatorum*.

Fig. 2. In this illustration from Jean de Papeleu's *Bible historiée* (1317), Christ in the heavenly city extends his blessing while holding in his left hand the world in the form of a medieval T-and-O map.

12

churches, and the poem come to light.[13] It can be seen that the reader-actor is almost invariably directed by the corresponding forms of pilgrimage typology from a re-enacted Exodus conversion of the soul from sin to grace, to a Redemption of the soul through figured reception of Christ, to a Transfiguration of the soul through figured visions of the elect and of God.[14]

Past studies have revealed how the sequence of Dante's actions beyond life are joined through figural "back references" to events recorded in the Bible, to corresponding pilgrimage events scored in the iconographic Book of the World, and to personal episodes in Dante's own *Vita Nuova*. The poet's *Vita Nuova*, a book of personal remembered history, discloses a pattern of prefiguring personal events associated through typology to biblical episodes, from which the fulfilling other-worldly pilgrimage of Dante arises.[15] The *Vita Nuova* recounts the love of Dante for Beatrice as a type

---

[13] For accounts of the long pilgrimage recorded in an international body of pilgrim texts, see the fine compendium of twelfth and thirteenth-century texts recently gathered together with notes by Franciscan editor Sabino de Sandoli in *Itinera Hierosolymitana Crucesignatorum*, vol. 1 (Jerusalem, 1978); vol. 2 (Jerusalem, 1980), with the third volume forthcoming. Thanks are due Sabino de Sandoli for making the galleys of the third volume available to me. A bibliography of medieval French pilgrim texts on the Exodus route, published by the French Oriental Institute, appears in Mahfouz Labib's *Pèlerins et Voyageurs au Mont Sinai* (Cairo, 1961). A great variety of representative Holy Land pilgrimage narratives have been collected in *Itinéraires à Jérusalem et Descriptions de la Terre Sainte*, ed. Henri Michelant and Gaston Raynoud (Geneva, 1882); *Itinera Hierosolymitana et Descriptiones Terrae Sanctae*, ed. Titus Tobler and Augustus Molinier (Osnabruck, 1966); *Itinéraires Russes en Orient*, ed. B. De Khitrowo (Osnabruck, 1966); and *Deutsche Pilgerreisen nach dem Heiligen Lande*, ed. Reinhold Rohricht (Osnabruck, 1967). For selected narratives of medieval English pilgrims to the Holy Land, along with a bibliography of medieval pilgrim texts published in English, see Franciscan editor Eugene Hoade's *Western Pilgrims* (Jerusalem, 1952).

[14] In an incisive exposition affording insight into Dante's processional pilgrimage typology based in part upon the Book of God's Words, the Scriptures, Georges Duby in *The Age of the Cathedrals* points out that "history was a song of glory . . . fitted into the liturgy." Universal history, he notes, was conceived as unfolding in "one continuous procession." He adds that "the Scriptures, which were no different from a history, described it [universal history] as a gradual ascension in three phases. The New Testament—the second phase—had smoothed out the rough spots that remained in humankind during the first phase, prior to the Incarnation. . . . The processions to and within the abbey churches were symbolic realizations of history. They completed the last phase as they mimed the entry into the Kingdom of Heaven" (pp. 79–80). For an account of the influence of Jerusalem pilgrimage traditions on the medieval liturgy, particularly in Rome, see Johan Chydenius, "The Typological Problem in Dante," 70–86. The figurism of Holy Land places and events, as expressed in medieval liturgy and then reflected in the *Commedia*, is analyzed by Fr. Dunstan Tucker, "The *Divine Comedy* and the Liturgy of Holy Week," *Orate Fratres* 14 (1940): 204–211; "Baptism in Dante's *Purgatorio*," *Orate Fratres* 15 (1940): 112–122; and by Lizette Andrews Fisher, *The Mystic Vision in the Grail Legend and in the Divine Comedy* (New York, 1917), 87–116. See also the study of the development of religious ritual from pilgrimage traditions in Chapter XVI, "Mediaeval Christianity: Religion to Ritual" in Jonathan Sumption, *Pilgrimage: An Image of Medieval Religion* (Totowa, New Jersey, 1975), 289–302.

[15] Referring to classical and medieval rhetorical works on the poetic uses of memory, Barbara Nolan in "The *Vita Nuova*: Dante's Book of Revelation," *Dante Studies* 88 (1970), shows how Dante as narrator "first of all aligns the story of his love for Beatrice with the pattern of Old and New Testament accounts of man's gradual growth in love and knowledge of God"; and then by disclosing his "personal history, in Florence over the course of fifteen years, participates

of Christ, his spiritual separation and "turn" from his lady after her death, and his partial spiritual regeneration through consciousness of pilgrims and especially of Palmers and Romers.

In the manner of medieval religious buildings with earthly types below and heavenly anti-types above, Dante constructed the *Commedia* from two figurally related but reversed points of view. The heavenly inceptive cause of the poem, Dante's experience of a vision inspired by Beatrice in the Empyrean, is recorded in final Chapter XLIII of the *Vita Nuova* in which the poet tells of a "miraculous vision in which I saw things that made me resolve to say nothing further of this most blessed one, until a time when I could discourse more worthily about her" ("mirabil visione, nella quale vidi cose, che me fecero proporre di non dir più di questa benedetta, infino a tanto che io potessi più degnamente trattare di lei").[16]

The earthly cause of the *Commedia* is Dante's awareness, in Chapter XLI, of the pilgrimage of Romers through Beatrice's city on their way to Old St. Peter's Basilica in the eternal city to view the Veil of Veronica: the "blessed portrait left to us by Jesus Christ as a copy of his most beautiful face" ("imagine benedetta, la quale Gesù Cristo lasciò a noi per esempio della sua bellissima figura"). This earthly pilgrimage to Rome suddenly stirs Dante to conceive of a sonnet "Oltre la spera" ("Beyond the Sphere") describing the pilgrimage of his "sospiro" or sigh to Beatrice in heaven. The sigh charts the other-worldly pathway that Dante will someday take in the *Paradiso*, ascending through the spheres to the Empyrean where it gazes upon Beatrice who in turn is looking upon God.

Dante in Chapter XLI then reflects upon the different kinds of travelers, including those who are known as "peregrini" going to the shrine of St. James in Galicia; he writes of those whose journeys, when joined, comprise the full great circle pilgrimage. According to the poet, "They are called Palmers who go beyond the sea eastward, whence they often bring back palm-branches" ("Chiamansi *Palmieri* in quanto vanno, oltremare lá onde

---

by imitation in the cosmic history of salvation" (p. 53). Cast in "figurative, enigmatic revelations," this personal history, she writes, is a demonstration of "human memory discovering meaning in history" and "indicates directions which point unmistakably to the *Commedia*" (pp. 51, 53, 76). Marianne Shapiro in "Figurality in the *Vita Nuova*: Dante's New Rhetoric," *Dante Studies* 97 (1979), further discusses Dante's rhetorical techniques and figural participation in biblical history, including the Christological typology of the *peregrino spirito* of sonnet XLI in the *Vita Nuova*, in reading the work primarily as an "allegory of the theologians" (pp. 107–127). V. A. Kolve in *Chaucer and the Imagery of Narrative: The First Five Canterbury Tales* (Stanford, 1984), 9–58, cites Dante, among many other medieval authors, in presenting illustrations of how medieval writers employed memory in their selection and disposition of imagery. Dante, Kolve observes, uses "images born of sense experience with the secular world" in creating an allegory of "multivalent significance" that is "anchored in history" (pp. 46, 296). See also Phillip H. Wicksteed, *From Vita Nuova to Paradiso: Two Essays on the Vital Relations between Dante's Successive Works* (London and New York, 1922), for general remarks on two "visions" of Dante, one at the end of the *Vita Nuova* and the other at the end of *Paradiso*.

[16] All quotations of the *Vita Nuova* are from *Le Opere di Dante Alighieri*, ed. E. Moore, rev. Paget Toynbee, 4th ed. (Oxford, 1924).

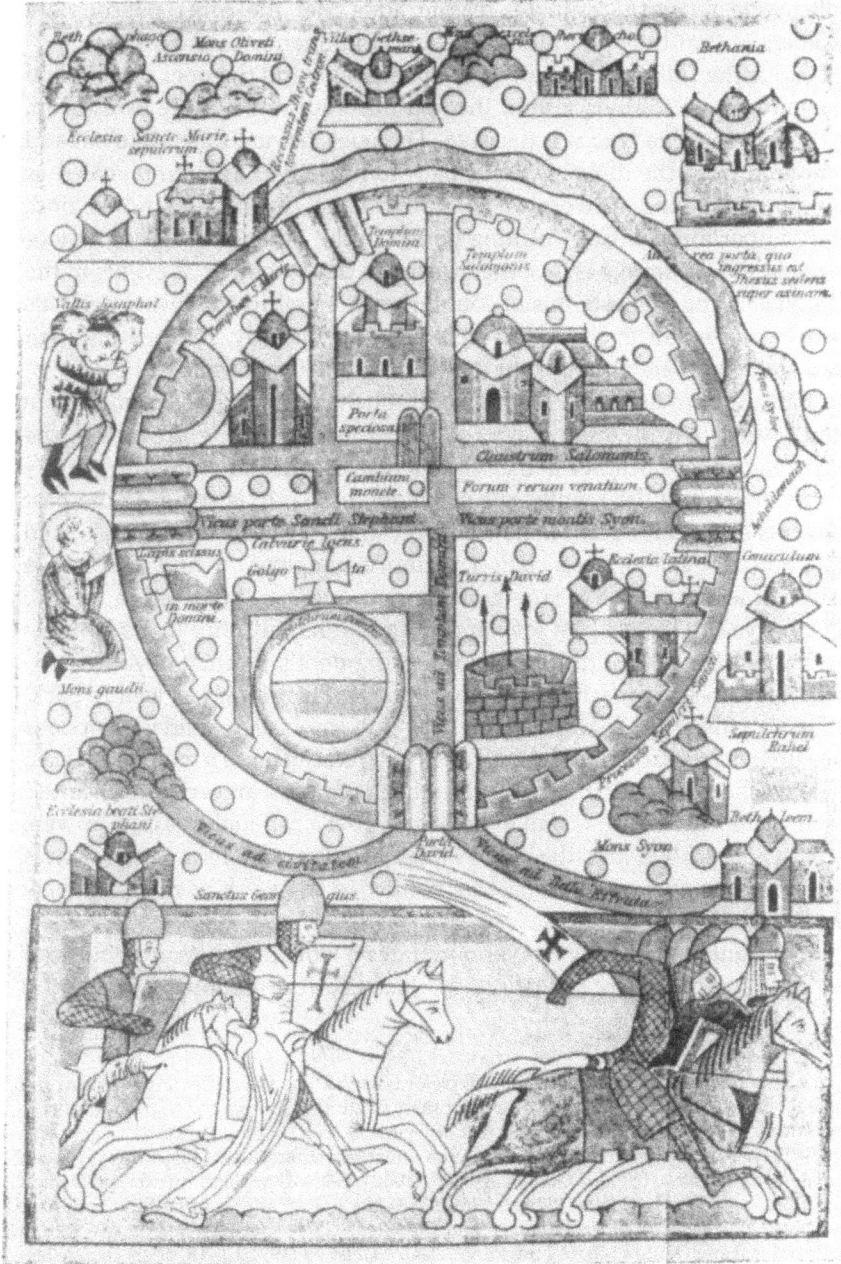

FIG. 4. Several "stations" of the Redemption near the Holy Sepulchre's circular Anastasis, divided here with T-and-O type zonal lines, are depicted in this crusader map of Jerusalem (ca. 1170).

molte volte recano la palma"). Dante adds that the other pilgrims are "Romers in that they go to Rome" ("*Romei* in quanto vanno a Roma").

Despite the fulfilling journey of the poet's sigh and the poet's brief, final allusion to a mysterious vision, the spiritual "turn" of Dante away from Beatrice in the *Vita Nuova* is decisive. The poet, having fallen into sin and wandered from the direct spiritual path to his lady, has been revealed as going on an extended twofold "long pilgrimage" in this life and beyond. Every important spiritual "turning point" in the other-worldly journey of Dante in the *Commedia* is in some measure a development of events in the *Vita Nuova;* for example, his encounter with Virgil in the low desert, his "turn" on the hair of Satan toward Eden and his lady, his meeting with dead souls who are about to climb Mt. Purgatory, his vision of Beatrice in the Earthly Paradise, his growing comprehension from the height of the fixed stars of earthly pilgrimage routes below, his gazing upward in the Empyrean toward Beatrice in the celestial rose. Again and again the memory of the reader and, frequently but belatedly, of Dante is swept to the past as events beyond life recur in new and yet strangely familiar patterns. Then in a flood of revelatory association, memory, imagination, and reason take a sudden leap, and the meaning of the new event is illumined in the full perspective of Dante's past love and changing relationship to his lady. At the same time, every "turning point" in the poet's journey beyond is inevitably related, by means of typology that points forward as well as back, to Dante's vision of Beatrice in the heavenly rose as she guides the poet's eyes upward toward God. In the Earthly Paradise Dante's memory of past sin is washed away in the river Lethe. In the Empyrean certain of Dante's lesser faculties weaken or fail even as the poet's rational intuitive powers increase. But throughout, the poet's imitative figural actions and experiences in themselves give an interrelated structure to the work as it successively unfolds before the reader.

How Dante's pilgrimage beyond imitates events in the World Book and the Bible has been precisely charted.[17] Just as a foreshadowing Palmer on

---

[17] A detailed reading of Dante's full Egypt-Jerusalem-Rome Great Circle pilgrimage and biblical typology, together with references to primary pilgrimage sources and related scholarship and criticism, appears in the notes and text of Demaray, *The Invention of Dante's Commedia,* pp. 9–92, 133–185. This study is an elaboration of earlier publications: "Pilgrim Text Models for Dante's *Purgatorio,*" *Studies in Philology* (Jan., 1969): 1–25; "The Pilgrim Texts and Dante's Three Beasts, *Inferno* I," *Italica* (Winter, 1969): 233–241; and "Patterns of Earthly Pilgrimage in Dante's *Commedia:* Palmers, Romers, and the Great Circle Journey." Carol V. Kaske in "Mount Sinai and Dante's Mount Purgatory," *Dante Studies* 79 (1971): 1–18, offers an excellent interpretation, referring to past figural studies including the work of A. C. Charity, of the typological relationship of Mt. Sinai and Mt. Purgatory. See also the early study by Rodolfo Benini: "Il grande Sion, il Sinai e il piccolo Sion," *Rendiconti della Reale Accademia dei Lincei,* 5th ser. 23: 1–25, in which the author presents original but somewhat impressionistic readings, using medieval geographical writings but not pilgrim texts, in arguing that Mt. Purgatory is modeled after a partly mythical, partly geographical "Grand Sion," a mountain that was thought to rise to the sphere of the moon and that was composed of the combined peaks of Horeb, Pharan, and Sinai. Interpretations of Dante's journey up Mt. Purgatory have been related to the biblical Exodus by Charles Singleton, particularly in " 'In Exitu Israel de Aegypto,' "

earth in the pilgrimage year of 1300 moves "uphill" from worldly Egypt over the Sinai deserts, past a "gate of confession" and up the stone terraces and steps of Mt. Sinai, and on to the geographic center of the northern hemisphere at Jerusalem; so Dante in an other-worldly re-enactment of the Exodus journey moves uphill over a desert strand, past a gate of confession and up the stone terraces and steps of Mt. Purgatory, and on to a summit Eden situated at the geographic center of the southern hemisphere. Then in a fulfillment of the presaging terrestrial movement of a Palmer to the temple, tomb, and cross of Redemption on the Jerusalem pilgrimage way of the cross, Dante in Eden moves to figural representations of the Jerusalem temple, tomb, and cross in encountering Beatrice, a type of Christ. Finally, just as a prefiguring Palmer—now taking the name Romer—on a pilgrimage of return sails through the waters and reflected light of the Mare Internum to the shore near Rome, and then traverses the stations of the eternal city to the gate and tomb of St. Peter and to the relic of the Veil of Veronica; so too Dante, acting out the journey in part through inverted typal correspondences, soars through the light of "the great sea of being" (*Par.* I, 113; "lo gran mar de l'essere") to a "riva" or shore of right love (*Par.* XXVI, 63), and then experiences transfiguring visions of a heavenly eternal city that are compared to the experiences of travelers to Rome.

Past studies have also shown how, within the recurrent narrative of the *Commedia*, each of the three central biblical events re-enacted in the world beyond is foreshadowed within the patterned action of a preceding other-worldly event.[18] When Dante is driven backward after his attempted ascent of the delectable mountain in *Inferno* I, it is within the matrix of this failed Exodus pilgrimage action, prefiguring later true figured Exodus pilgrimage on Mt. Purgatory, that Dante learns of Beatrice's intercession with Virgil in the vestibule of hell. Beatrice's descent to the vestibule presages Dante's figured Redemption before Beatrice in Eden. Then within the Redemptive pattern of action in the Earthly Paradise, Dante sees a miraculous tree that renews itself in a prefiguration of the Transfiguration. Having fallen asleep

---

Seventy-Eighth Annual Report of the Dante Society (1960); 1–24; and by Fr. Dunstan J. Tucker, " 'In Exitu Israel de Aegypto': *The Divine Comedy* in the Light of the Easter Liturgy," *The American Benedictine Review* 11 (March–June, 1960): 43–61. See too Singleton's " 'Sulla fiumana ove 'l mar non ha vanto'," *The Romanic Review* 39 (December, 1948): 269–277; and John Freccero's "The River of Death: *Inferno* II, 108" in *The World of Dante: Six Studies in Language and Thought*, ed. S. Bernard Chandler and J. A. Molinaro (Toronto, 1966), 26–41.

Among studies associating the *Commedia* with the Jubilee Pilgrimage of 1300 are C. Carboni, *Il Giubileo di Bonifazio VIII e la Commedia di Dante* (Roma, 1901); R. Zingarelli, *Dante e Roma* (Roma, 1895); Lonsdale Ragg, *Dante and His Italy* (New York and London, 1907); Thomas Caldecot Chubb, *Dante and His World* (Boston and Toronto, 1966), 23–46; Fr. Herbert Thurston, *The Holy Year of Jubilee* (Westminster, Maryland, 1949), 10–27; William Anderson, *Dante the Maker*, 152, 278–381; Julia Bolton Holloway, "Dante's *Commedia*: Egyptian Spoils, Roman Jubilee, and Florence's Patron," *Studies In Medieval Culture* 12 (1978): 97–104; and Peter Armour, *The Door of Purgatory.*

[18] See Demaray, "Invention from the Book of God's Words," *The Invention of Dante's Commedia*, 116–131.

before the tree, the poet compares his spiritual illumination upon awakening to that of the three Apostles on Mt. Tabor (*Purg.* XXXII, 38–60, 73–84). Dante begins his own Transfiguration in the stars in the presence of the manifested hosts of Christ Triumphant, hosts to some degree prefigured in Eden through the procession representing Books of the Bible and the earthly Church Militant. Among the stars Dante sees and speaks to the Apostles of the Transfiguration, his spiritual revelations in this realm pre-showing his final Transfiguration before the Cosmic Book ingathered in God.

During visionary encounters of Dante with his lady that are also pivotal junctures in the figural design of the *Commedia*—the final Exodus pilgrimage conversion of the poet before Beatrice in Eden; his later Redemption before his lady also in the Garden; and his interior Transfiguration initially inspired by gazing upon Beatrice in the celestial rose—the poet has been observed to call conspicuous attention to his three primary "source books": the Bible, the Cosmic Book that includes the World Book, and the *Vita Nuova.* By moving his own and his reader's consciousness backward and forward by alluding to foreshadowed and realized events signified in these three "source books," he provides through the "operation" of his figurism an index to just where in the twofold pilgrimage he has been, where he is in the remembered "present" of his peregrinations, and where he has yet to go.

Dante's awareness of famed "World Book" typology associated with Redemption in Jerusalem and Transfiguration in Rome can be readily understood, it seems to me, by modern readers. Yet because the fifteenth-century geographic revolution dramatically displaced Mt. Sinai and other Exodus sites from their preeminent locations near the medieval world's "center," readers and commentators, accustomed to modern maps of Italy and the Mediterranean basin in recent editions of the *Commedia,* may find it somewhat difficult to appreciate the earlier and very different typological outlook of Dante and his contemporaries toward the Exodus pilgrimage route and the legendary thundering mountain of God.

In Dante's period biblical and worldly typology were inseparable. As early as the sixth century, the Sinai monk Cosmas Indicopleustes in his influential *Topographia Christiana* had illustrated geographical-biblical "truth" by placing Jerusalem at the world's geographic center, and the Sinai sites close to that center. By the eighth century, psalters and biblical commentaries were regularly illustrated with world T-and-O maps of the Sallust and Beatus type showing the Sinai area next to the central Holy City. From the tenth through the thirteenth centuries, world T-and-O maps culminating in the detailed projections by Isidore of Seville, Henry of Mainz, Richard of Haldingham, and the creator of the Epsdorf world chart regularly included triangular drawings of Mt. Sinai on the sometimes-marked Exodus path leading through the Red Sea or to Jerusalem at the center.

The fifteenth-century empirical geographical revolution, transformed Mt. Sinai from a famed spiritual-geographic "type" near the center of the world into a merely physical topographical "feature" now far-removed toward the equator somewhere at the southern tip of the Sinai peninsula. Following the crusades, western pilgrims in considerable numbers continued to visit the thundering mountain of God. It was therefore left to the sixteenth-century Protestant Reformation attack upon the veneration of relics and pilgrimage sites largely to end the traditional importance of Mt. Sinai as a type and a "station" on the actual pilgrimage pathway to Jerusalem. The Reformation also helped to create the nearly total modern breach, based upon evolving doctrinal and cultural differences, between the Greek monastic establishment at Mt. Sinai and the Latin West.

THE TEMPLES, LABYRINTHS, AND ROSES OF EARTH

Although Dante demonstrates in the *Commedia* a comprehensive knowledge of Great Circle pilgrimage typology doubtless variously gained from pilgrimage literature and Patristic commentary, from world T-and-O icons containing illustrations of Mt. Sinai and selected Holy Land stations, and from the pilgrimage and crusading oral traditions fostered by the Franciscans, the Knights Templar, and other groups, the poet inevitably was influenced by the pilgrimage art and architecture of medieval churches. What immediately and powerfully confronted Dante as an Italian artist of the late Middle Ages was the international Byzantine-Romanesque-Gothic iconography of long pilgrimage, an iconography richly manifest as part of a living pilgrimage tradition through art works in the "temples" and churches of Florence, Bologna, Pisa, Rome, Venice, Ravenna, Assisi, and other Italian and northern European cities. Though modes of architectural figurism and iconography differed, the major kinds of religious buildings—the round churches or "temples" largely developed in form from Constantine's Holy Sepulchre, the rectangular Romanesque basilicas adapted from the design of imperial Roman law courts, and the cruciform stone-and-glass Gothic cathedrals constructed to receive and project heavenly light—all contained figured long pilgrimage "stations" and altars and relics signifying, with varying degrees of comprehensiveness, foreshadowing earthly and fulfilled heavenly personages, objects, and realms. In Gothic cathedrals elaborate stone structural systems and structured wheel-rose windows to a large degree replaced Byzantine mosaics and paintings as types for the earthly and the eternal. However, even the famed Byzantine "temple" of the Holy Sepulchre, as described in pilgrim texts after the sixth century elaborating upon the fourth-century account of Eusebius Pamphila, embodied cosmic typology in the structural signification of its perfect-circle Resurrection building or Anastasis, its Anastasis hemisphere covering or dome, and its central tomb surrounded by what Eusebius claimed were twelve pilasters representing the Apostles.[19]

---

[19] *Life of Constantine*, trans. John H. Bernard, intro. and notes T. Hayter Lewis (London, 1896), 8–9.

In criticism relating medieval architectural elements to Dante's poem of pilgrimage, the fascinating issue of the comparative pilgrimage origins, typology, and figural structures of both the *Commedia* and of early "temples" and churches has yet to be seriously explored. It was in the fourth century that the first Christian Emperor Constantine, it should be recalled, constructed for the use of pilgrims the round Anastasis—or possibly a semicircular Anastasis definitely reported as round in the seventh century and later—after his mother Helena "discovered" key stations and relics while on Holy Land pilgrimage. The circular design of the Anastasis was then reflected in the circular ground plan with octagonal outer walls of the Dome-of-the-Rock Sanctuary (Kubbet-es-Sakhra) in Jerusalem, erected in the temple area of the city in the seventh century, and associated by pilgrims with the Old Temple of Solomon. In Rome during the fourth century, Constantine is credited with building the basilicas of Old St. Peter's, Old St. Paul's, St. John Lateran and other churches both to house the tombs of apostles, saints, and imperial relatives—many of whom had traveled to the eternal city from the Holy Land—but also according to tradition to contain Exodus and Passion relics supposedly carried to Rome by Helena.[20] In France during the mid-twelfth century, Abbot Suger, who stated in his *De Administratione* that he regularly conversed with travelers from Jerusalem, constructed the "first" Gothic cathedral, St. Denis, as a royal pilgrimage and crusading center thus, in the words of architectural critic and historian Otto von Simson, "linking the religious heart of France with Jerusalem, the navel of the world."[21]

Worshippers in the round churches, basilicas, and cathedrals moved over the earthly nave floor, or through ambulatories, to the high altar usually signifying temple altars at Jerusalem. At St. Maria in Aquiro and St. Maria in Trastevere in Rome; St. Vitale and St. Giovanni Evangelista, Ravenna; St. Martino, Lucca; San Giovanni al Sepolcro, Brindisi; St. Savino, Piacenza; and at Amiens; Rheims; Chartres; Sens; St. Michele Maggiore, Pavia; Bayeux; Poitiers and a host of other medieval churches, inlaid stone

---

[20] Vergilio C. Corbo in *Il Santo Sepolcro di Gerusalemme: Aspetti archaelogici dalle origini al periodo crociato,* 2 vols. (Jerusalem, 1981) presents a reconstruction of the fourth-century Anastasis or Rotunda of the Holy Sepulchre, based on recent excavations and early texts, in the form of a circular nave within a lower ambience, semicircular in the back and rectangular in front. (See the outlined reconstruction in vol. 2, Tavola 3.) After examining the site and the evidence, however, this writer agrees with reservations about Corbo's proposed plan offered by Richard Krautheimer in the Postscript to "Santo Stefano Rotondo and the Holy Sepulchre Rotunda," *Studies In Early Christian, Medieval, and Renaissance Art* (New York and London, 1969): namely, that "this reconstruction is so contrary to the descriptions beginning with Egeria's in the late fourth century and continuing with Arculf's that . . . the results of further examination of the structure" should be awaited (p. 105).

See the discussions, supported by illustrations, of the Near Eastern Byzantine influence on the processional-pilgrimage designs of medieval European round churches, basilicas, and cathedrals in André Grabar, *Martyrium,* 3 vols.; Richard Krautheimer, *Studies in Early Christian, Medieval, and Renaissance Art;* G. Bandmann, *Mittelalterliche Architektur als Bedeutungstrager* (Berlin, 1951); and Otto von Simson, *The Gothic Cathedral.*

[21] *The Gothic Cathedral,* 81.

labyrinth nave floors or labyrinths carved in stone contained intervolved, directional pathways that pointed worshippers to a central rose or other medallion usually representing, particularly in church pilgrimage iconography of the thirteenth and fourteenth centuries, the fulfilled and "true" spiritual-geographic "station" of Jerusalem.[22]

A number of the core medallions were scored, within containing floral or geometric iconographic forms, with small minotaur and pagan icons signifying the "old" spiritual-geographic centers of Crete or Troy, foreshadowing types of the "new" Hebraic-Christian center of the Holy City. The minotaur at the core of labyrinths served too as an icon indicating a spiritual-geographic center of evil in the underworld, a foreshadowing type of hell and the figural antithesis of the Holy City. The mazes in their entirety quite clearly represented this earthly world; and in their architectural configurations, they appear also to have suggested a prefiguring antithetical or corresponding pagan form for the fulfilled and transcending "temple" architecture of Jerusalem; and through wider typological association, for the Christian church architecture of Europe.[23]

Some medieval worshippers could have shown contempt for evil and this world by stepping upon mazes marked with the minotaur. Still, in

---

[22] See Hermann Kern's comprehensive *Labyrinthe* (Munich, 1982), particularly the chapter "Kirchen-Labyrinthe" (206–218). A catalog of known medieval church labyrinths is provided together with photographs and drawings of various designs (pp. 219–241). Included too is a catalog of known labyrinths of the Chartres type (p. 211), and a chapter on medieval church and outdoor labyrinths in Great Britain (pp. 243–253). See also Paolo Santarcangeli, *Le livre des labyrinthes: Histoire d'un mythe et d'un symbole*, trans. from the Italian by Monique Lacau (Paris, 1974), 272–301. Santarcangeli gives accounts of inlaid stone labyrinth floors over which medieval pilgrims and sometimes holy ritualistic dancers were believed to have moved in figured imitation of Exodus or divine peregrinations to the earthly and heavenly Jerusalem (pp. 215–220, 296–298). Because as Santarcangeli notes many of these floors in France and elsewhere were destroyed during religious wars and during the French Revolution, the full number once existing cannot be accurately fixed. Santarcangeli records the dates of the construction and destruction of important labyrinths; for example, Amiens, built in 1288, destroyed in 1828; Rheims, ca. 1240, destroyed in 1779; Chartres, uncertain date, still existing; Sens, uncertain date, now destroyed; Arras, uncertain date, destroyed in 1779; Auxerre, uncertain date, destroyed in 1769; Bayeux, uncertain date, now destroyed; Poitiers, uncertain date, now destroyed; Canterbury, uncertain date, now destroyed; Abbey of Toussaints à Châlons-sur-Marne, uncertain date, destroyed in 1544; Abbey of Saint-Étienne à Caen, uncertain date, destroyed in 1802. Evidence suggests that the cathedral of Saint-Omer, and two and possibly three churches in Cologne, may each respectively have contained a labyrinth. See also the description and photographs of the twelfth-century world T-and-O mosaic map in the floor of the romanesque Church of St. Salvatore, Turin, materials published by Ernst Kitzinger, "The World Map and Fortune's Wheel: A Medieval Mosaic Floor in Turin," *Proceedings of the American Philosophical Society* 117, no. 5 (Oct. 1973): 344–373.

[23] See William H. Matthews, *Mazes and Labyrinths: Their History and Development* (New York, 1970), reprinted from the 1922 edition, 65–68, for speculations on the possible medieval uses and significations of church labyrinths. Erwin Panofsky in *Early Netherlandish Painting: Its Origin and Character*, vol. 1 (Cambridge, Mass., 1964), 132–139, though not directly commenting upon labyrinths, points out how in late medieval and Renaissance paintings and illuminations new Gothic structures were represented as arising from the depicted earthly ruins of earlier pagan or other constructions. It should be noted that even pilgrim Dante, on Mt. Purgatory's terrace of the proud, walks upon sculpture showing the ruins of Troy (*Purg.* XII, 61–69).

many pilgrimage churches the lowly floor labyrinths, through their directional pathways, would doubtless have conveyed to medieval worshippers, not only a sense of a single journey, but also a sense of a hierarchy of earthly journeys to an evil and to holy spiritual-geographic centers, with the earthly Exodus pilgrimage to Jerusalem the fulfillment of prefiguring pagan travels. By tracing or moving over "true" labyrinth paths leading to central floral, circular, or otherwise geometrically-shaped containing medallions, pilgrim-worshippers on nave floors, after confessing their sins, could have re-enacted *in figura* on the higher plane of fulfillment the wandering journey of conversion through the maze of this world to the Holy City. Given the dimensions, the apparent typological function, and the iconographic positioning of the largest of the circular or otherwise geometrical floor labyrinths in pilgrimage churches such as those at Rheims and Chartres—labyrinths extending completely across the main aisles not far from entrance portals—it seems very likely, as commentators have long suggested but have been unable conclusively to prove, that medieval pilgrims actually fell to their knees on the mazes and so acted out figural journeys to Jerusalem before rising and proceeding down the aisles to main altars.

Inscriptions preserved on extant reproductions of two central "station" medallions identify church architects. Jean d'Obais, first Master Builder of Rheims, and Robert Luzarches, first Master Builder of Amiens, have their names and those of their immediate successors "humbly" scored at the center of the labyrinths in their respective cathedrals, thus apparently signifying that they have built fulfilled types of Hebraic-Christian "temples" transcending foreshadowing pagan structures of the past, and that they have *in figura* reached the "new" earthly world center of Jerusalem and yet have remained in a lowly spiritual position. Recent studies of the inlaid and carved church labyrinths, particularly the inclusive work of Hermann Kern who discusses fifty-one such church structures in Italy, northern Europe, and Britain, reveal how numerous and popular were these figural pathways to foreshadowing "old" pagan centers and to the earthly Holy City, a type for the heavenly city of God.

Writing of the great cathedral of Chartres in which Dante's last guide in the *Commedia*, the mystic St. Bernard of Clairvaux, had accepted leadership, at the urging of Abbot Suger, of the planned third crusade to Jerusalem, architectural critic Painton Cowen presents a striking but unelaborated comment on the cathedral's giant 13.36-meter west wheel-rose window; the cathedral's huge, circular 12,885-meter inlaid stone labyrinth in the nave floor; and the pilgrimage of Dante in the *Commedia*.

Below the rose is the labyrinth, set into the nave at such distance from the west door that if the rose were to be "hinged down" it would almost fit over it. Labyrinths generally symbolize the path of the soul through life, and medieval pilgrims re-enacted this, following the path of the labyrinth in the cathedral on their knees, symbolizing the journey to Jerusalem. The rose window superimposed on this labyrinth suggests the mandala, the viewfinder of meaning, projected on to life, as a means not only of finding one's way but also of differentiating between the forces of good and evil. In the *Divine Comedy* we can see identical symbolism in Dante's journey through the spheres of Hell, Purgatory and Paradise on a journey that, he himself says, could be interpreted four different ways, one of which was that of the Christian through life. On arrival at the last circle of Paradise, Beatrice offers Dante a rose; so too at Chartres the labyrinth weaves its way (there is only one path) through concentric circles and at the centre there is a six-petalled rosette into which the path leads: it unmistakably echoes the rosette at the centre of the rose window that overlooks it.[24]

In Italy in Dante's period, circular twelfth-century labyrinths of the Chartres design existed in churches in Lucca, Pavia, and Piacenza and in St. Maria in Aquiro, Rome; and a drawing of a Chartres-type labyrinth illustrates a manuscript copy of the *Commedia* (ca. 1419) now in the Vatican library.[25]

---

[24] *Rose Windows* (San Francisco, 1979), 98–99. See also Santarcangeli, *Le livre des labyrinthes*, 291–292. The Chartres labyrinth was known to medieval pilgrims as the "station of Jerusalem." A ninth-century manuscript from the Abbey of Saint-Germain-des-Prés contains a drawing of an identical labyrinth with a minotaur at the center, thus leading to speculation that in early times the Chartres labyrinth may also have signified the pathway to the pagan world center at Crete.

Jean Vilette in "L'énigme du labyrinthe," *Notre-Dame de Chartres* 58 (March, 1984): 4–12, has recently called attention to the figural relation of the west wheel-rose and the labyrinth. Even the size of the two structures, he notes, is similar, for the labyrinth is only about half a meter smaller in diameter than the rose window. John James in "Chartres: Les constructeurs," *Société Archéologique d'Eure-et-Loir* 3 (1982), finds the labyrinth a second axis of the church nave corresponding in ground plan to the main axis at the intersection of nave and transept (p. 206).

Labyrinth designs, as Kern in *Labyrinthe* points out (pp. 206–218), lead to medallions or hubs sometimes signifying *in figura* unholy as well as holy centers. The focal point of journey can sometimes be interpreted as representing in hierarchical order the center of hell or the underworld; the old pagan center of Troy; the later pagan center of Crete; and on a higher level of figural fulfillment, the "true" spiritual-geographic center of the earthly Jerusalem, a type for the heavenly city.

Dante in the *Commedia* reflects a traditional medieval view of earthly directional figurism evident in the labyrinths, but the poet causes this earthly directional figurism to converge on the city of Rome as a center and goal. Dante in his poem states that he will follow in the footsteps of Aeneas who in the *Aeneid* is described as journeying from Troy to the eternal city (*Inf.* II, 20–33). Dante refers also to the statue of an Old Man signifying humanity standing at the pagan center of Crete, a statue with eyes turned toward Rome but with shoulders pointing toward Egyptian Damietta (*Inf.* XIV, 103–120). Studies have shown how the shoulders indicate a traditional crusading-pilgrimage pathway, one followed even by St. Francis, to or past the old pagan world center to Damietta and then to the Holy Land. The statue faces the final goal of long pilgrimage: Rome.

See Rodolfo Benini, "Il grande Sion, il Sinai e il piccolo Sion," *Rendiconti della Reale Accademia dei Lincei*, 5th ser. 23 (Roma, 1915): 8–10; Demaray, *Invention*, 150–154; and Anderson, *Dante the Maker*, 290–293. See also Anderson's diagram of the statue and the travel route to Jerusalem via Crete, Damietta, and Mt. Sinai; and to Rome from Jerusalem or Troy (p. 292, fig. 13).

Church labyrinth figurism can be seen in a general way as an analogue to Dante's labyrinth-like circular hell arranged in tiers leading down to Satan, and to the more ordered circular terraces of Mt. Purgatory leading up to an Eden figuring Jerusalem. However, the poet's movements in Eden and soaring ascent through the spheres both fulfills and transcends the figurism of nave labyrinth designs, and, in developing further analogues, the wider earthly and cosmic figurism of churches needs to be examined.

[25] Kern, *Labyrinthe*, p. 211. The manuscript of the *Commedia* is cataloged in the Vatican Library as Ms. Barb. Lat. 4112, fo. 209r.

A limited figural analogue, however, will later be substituted for Cowen's sweeping symbolic identification. Cathedral wheel-rose windows and related nave-floor labyrinths will be seen as figural elements generally similar, but not identical, to heavenly and earthly types in the *Commedia;* and movement over an earthly nave floor near entrance portals will be viewed as a type for only specified stages of a long twofold earthly and heavenly pilgrimage.

Worshippers at the main, figured "Jerusalem temple" altars in medieval churches received Christ in the form of the Eucharist and so acted out their Redemption by the Son. In Gothic cathedrals and basilicas of cruciform design, the main altar with crypt tomb underneath was located, of course, at the cross point of the nave and the transept or *bema* and, in Gothic structures, often orientated toward Jerusalem. Here at the Gothic "Jerusalem temple" altars the ritual of the reception of the Eucharist was performed between iconographic representations of the Books of the Old and New Testament. Old Testament biblical personages traditionally appeared in the cosmic wheel-rose of lesser radiance located in the north transept; New Testament personages in the cosmic wheel-rose made bright by direct sunlight in the south transept.[26]

In round churches the main altars rested at the centers of the circular naves usually over a crypt tomb, the plan being derived from pagan tomb and temple structures but also from the design of the "temple" of the Holy Sepulchre with Christ's altar tomb at the center of the round Anastasis.[27] The fifth-century church of Santo Stefano Rotondo in Rome takes this

---

[26] Cowen, *Rose Windows,* 8–10.

[27] See Corbo, *Il Santo Sepolcro di Gerusalemme.* Georges Duby in *The Age of the Cathedrals* rightly claims that the origins of European typological imitations of the "Temple" of the Holy Sepulchre can in large measure be traced to pilgrims. "When the pilgrims to the Holy Land arrived at their journey's end and entered the Holy Sepulchre," he writes, "the structure they entered was round. . . . Hence the popularity of this type of architecture. In the eleventh century it spread through the Empire as far as Slavic borders" (p. 24). In *Il S. Sepolcro Riprodotto in Occidente* (Jerusalem, 1971), Damiano Neri, examining the plethora of medieval figural imitations of the Holy Sepulchre built by the Knights Templar and others throughout Europe, maintains that by the eleventh century such construction projects had become a European "mania" (p. 95). Neri discusses the figural models of the Sepulchre erected in numerous Italian cities including Rome, Florence, Pisa, Bologna, Milan, and Borgo S. Sepolcro. Neri observes too that the Holy Sepulchre Ceremony of the Holy Fire, an Easter candle-lighting ceremony that commences in the cupola tomb of Christ at the center of the round Anastasis in Jerusalem, was imitated *in figura* annually at Easter in medieval Florence after pilgrims were said to have brought reports of the ceremony from the Holy Land (pp. 78–79).

In writing of the Knights' Templar constructions in Florence, Neri points out that the Knights were associated with an eleventh-century hospital with church attached near the Ponte Vecchio, and that two Florentine documents dated respectively 1189 and 1299 refer to a temple of the "Sancti Sepulcri" near the "Pontis Veteris" (pp. 68–69). In *Inf.* X, Dante, speaking to the heretical Florentine Farinata, remarks upon orations given in "nostro tempio," presumably the existing "temple" in their home city (1. 87).

See also George Jeffery's "The Holy Sepulchre in Jerusalem Reproduced as a Pilgrim Shrine in Europe," and "Lesser Copies of the Holy Sepulchre in different parts of Europe" in *A Brief Description of the Holy Sepulchre* (Cambridge, England, 1919), 195–219, 212–219.

circular form, as do in a general way the medieval figural imitations—
either round, hexagonal, or octagonal—of the Church of the Holy Sepulchre
at Pisa, Bologna, Milan, Borgo S. Sepolcro, Brindisi, and other Italian cities.
In sixth-century mosaics behind the main altar in the apse of St. Pudenziana,
Rome, the round Anastasis is directly represented along with other Jerusalem pilgrimage "stations" including Golgotha surmounted by the giant,
jeweled cross that was in fact erected on the site by Emperor Theodosius
I and later mentioned by the fourth-century pilgrim St. Silvia. These mosaics
signify too the heavenly Jerusalem by showing in the foreground an enthroned Christ in conclave with his disciples.[28]

At altars where worshippers acted out their Redemption, Passion relics
abounded. For example, Last Supper and a great variety of other relics, a
number of them said to have been brought to Rome by St. Helena, rested
in the *Sancta Sanctorum* altar in the Chapel of St. Lawrence, St. John Lateran.
The chapel was located in a separate hall of St. John Lateran that survived
the burning of the basilica in 1308. Fragments of the true cross, again
believed to have been carried to the eternal city by St. Helena, resided in
altars of the fourth century basilica of S. Croce di Gerusalemme, formerly
the Sessorian Palace, and were associated with the Jerusalem "station,"
within the Holy Sepulchre, of Helena's finding of the cross.[29]

Worshippers moving toward and gazing upon the lofty paintings or
mosaics or glowing wheel-rose windows often showing Christ at the center
of the Cosmos—icons fully visible only from the central main altars of the
"temples"—were then in a spiritual and physical position to attain *in figura*
a transfiguring vision of personages in the heavenly city and of God, a
figured vision reinforced by the holy ritualistic movements of clerics below
in typological imitation of the radiant images above that were often joined
in dynamic designs representing divine procession or circular dance. In the
eternal city of Rome, cosmic icons in Old St. Peter's Basilica, including a
sixth-century wheel-rose window, encircled the high altar of the supposed
Vicar of Christ, an altar located over the tomb of St. Peter and near spiral
columns said to be from the Temple of Solomon at this new western spiritual
center of the Latin Church.[30]

---

[28] See Jeffery's *A Brief Description*, 8–9, for an analysis of the St. Pudenziana mosaics in the
light of the pilgrimage tradition.

[29] See E. Venturini, *The Eternal City* (Roma, 1963), 108–116; Herbert Thurston, *The Holy
Year of Jubilee: An Account of the History and Ceremonial of the Roman Jubilee*, 171–197. The
location and appearance of sites and churches in Rome can be found in the work, translated
into several languages, and available in the French version entitled *Les Merveilles de la Ville
de Rome* (Roma, 1650). See also Constantine Carboni, *Il Giubileo di Bonifazio VIII e la Commedia
di Dante* (Roma, 1901); and the recent association of specific Jubilee Year 1300 pilgrimage
sites in Rome with Dante's rose of *Paradiso* in Peter Armour's *The Door of Purgatory: A Study
of Multiple Symbolism in Dante's Purgatorio*, 154–168.

[30] The design of Constantine's Old St. Peter's, together with an account of the rose window
added in the sixth century in the eastern facade, appears in James Lees-Milne's *Saint Peter's*
(London, 1967), 63–122. In Paul Letarouilly's *The Basilica of St. Peter* (London, 1953), an
analysis of the structure and ornamentation of the basilica is accompanied by plates (1 through

Worshippers in Old St. Peter's, engaging in a most spiritually transfiguring action considered a prefiguring earthly type for Beatific Vision, briefly
viewed at designated times, usually at the end of long pilgrimage, one of
the holiest relics in Christendom: the Veil of Veronica imprinted with the
visage of Christ. Writing of the Jubilee Pilgrimage of 1300, Giovanni Villani
observes that, during the period of the pilgrimage activities, "for the con-
solation of the Christian pilgrims, every Friday and every solemn feast day,
was shown in St. Peter's the Veronica, the true image of Christ, on the
napkin."[31]

In keeping with the practice of disclosing *in figura* at the center of pilgrimage "temples" some visual representation of transcendent religious
experience, the apses behind the main altars at SS. Cosma and Damiano,
Rome; of St. Apollinare in Classe and St. Vitale, Ravenna; and of many
smaller Byzantine-Romanesque churches shimmered with mosaics depicting the Transfiguration of Christ. These apse mosaics in Rome and Ravenna
have been found to be of the same style, technique, and period as the
sixth-century Transfiguration mosaics, with lateral Old Testament scenes
depicting Moses before the burning bush and receiving the Law, in the
apse of the Church of the Transfiguration, St. Catherine's Monastery, at
the base of the ring of pilgrimage "stations" on Mt. Sinai;[32] for in the
seventh century through Dante's period there was a steady and pronounced
communication over established land and sea routes between the international pilgrimage monastery and ring of "stations," controlled by Greek
monks, and the Latin West. The Church of the Transfiguration at Mt. Sinai
had its own chapel dedicated to SS. Cosma and Damiano, another chapel
reserved in Dante's time for the use of Latin pilgrims, and yet another
chapel dedicated to Constantine and also his mother Helena who by tradition had journeyed to Mt. Sinai as well as to Jerusalem and Rome.[33]

---

16) showing reconstructed elements of the edifice. See also the reconstruction of St. Peter's
as drawn by Frazer in Richard Krautheimer, *Studies in Early Christian, Medieval, and Renaissance
Art*, fig. 12; and the reconstruction by Alfarano in André Grabar, *Martyrium*, vol. 1, fig. 22,
with commentary, 293–305.
    [31] *Croniche Fiorentine*, 320.
    [32] Heinz Skobucha, *Sinai* (New York, London, and Toronto, 1966), 88–89.
    [33] Skobucha in *Sinai* discusses the chapels and offers evidence of the excellent relations
between the seventh-century Sinai bishop, John Climacus, and later bishops of Sinai and the
Papacy (pp. 78, 84, 94–98). In the seventh century Pope Gregory the Great corresponded
with Sinai Bishop John Climacus and warmly praised him; and in Dante's period Popes
Gregory X (1271–1276) and John XXII (1316–1334) both issued written statements renewing
the traditional Papal protection given to St. Catherine's Monastery and its possessions. Pope
John XXII alone produced eleven documents affirming his fatherly love for the Greek monks
of the monastery, and this Latin pope repeatedly supported in written briefs the rights of the
Greek monastery to property on Cyprus and Crete against the claims of the Venetians.
    The St. Catherine's Monastery and its legendary "angelic" desert monks rested secure in
a deep desert location beyond the bloody conflicts of the crusades and even somewhat removed
from Eastern and Western political and religious rivalries. This monastery, constructed largely
in the sixth century, had never been sacked; and it was unique in containing within its walls
a twelfth-century mosque and, in its library, a spurious firman from Mohammet granting
protection. At this famed pilgrimage center where clerics and pilgrims of different nationalities

Christ's Transfiguration on Mt. Tabor, as dramatically portrayed in Byzantine apse mosaics of pilgrimage churches at Mt. Sinai, Rome, Ravenna, and elsewhere and in a lancet window at Chartres, was *in figura* the recognized fulfillment of Old Testament events involving Moses on Mt. Sinai and New Testament events involving Christ on Mt. Sion. And these were the events respectively of the Exodus, Redemption, and Transfiguration that many worshippers in cathedrals and basilicas would have re-enacted during the Jubilee Pilgrimage Year of 1300, and at other times, in moving over earthly nave floors, receiving the Eucharist at main altars, and gazing upward upon mosaics or wheel-rose icons of Christ and His elect. They were the events too that Latin pilgrims on great circle journeys progressively acted out in seeking, first, spiritual conversion on the "stations" of the Exodus, next, Redemption on the "stations" of Jerusalem, and finally, Transfiguration through viewing the relic of the Veil of Veronica at St. Peter's on the "stations" of Rome.

Through references in the *Commedia* to that holy person who in life acted out the journey of the Israelites and the Passion and visionary illumination of the Son—"serafico" St. Francis—Dante presents an exemplum of sacred imitative conduct and demonstrates a knowledge of that pilgrimage mountain in Italy that served as a local type for those distant, hallowed mountains of the Exodus, Redemption, and Transfiguration in the Near East (*Par.* XI, 37). According to contemporaneous documents, St. Francis in fact made a pilgrimage from Damietta, Egypt, to the Holy Land in 1219–1220. Early in 1221 the saint journeyed to Rome. Then on Mount La Verna in Italy in September, 1224, in an extraordinary re-enactment of biblical events originally occurring on Mt. Sion and figurally associated Holy Land mountains, St. Francis is said to have fasted, prayed, and meditated forty days and forty nights before finally experiencing a vision of the crucifixion and being marked with the Stigmata. In November of 1224, the saint accompanied by his disciples traveled nineteen miles to the southeast from Mount La Verna to the medieval town of Borgo San Sepolcro, so named because it harbored yet another Italian figural reproduction of the temple

---

and cultures intermingled, language barriers were overcome as Copts, Greeks, Latins, Syrians, Russians and others shared common Exodus pilgrimage experiences in climbing the holy mountain of God. The pilgrimage pathways and carved rock steps leading from the monastery up terraced Mt. Sinai included in Dante's time a stone Gate of Confession through which pilgrims passed, sometimes confessing their sins to a guardian monk; a "ring" of Old Testament "stations" ascending to the supposed rock on which Moses received the Law; and even another summit rock supposedly scored by the hoof of Barac, the horse said in Sarah XVII of the *Koran* to have been ridden by Mohammet on his night journey to the seventh heaven. For here as at the medieval temple pilgrimage sites of Jerusalem, Hebraic, Christian, and Moslem traditions of holy "ascent" intermingled.

It is sometimes assumed that, because in the last few centuries there has been little cultural or artistic interchange between the Greek monastery of Mt. Sinai and the Latin West, there was little or none in earlier periods. Yet the body of Latin pilgrim texts from the fourth century through Dante's period—together with historical evidence of the surprisingly good relationship between Popes, Latin clerics and pilgrims, and the "heretical" but honored Greek desert fathers—suggests that such interchange was steady and influential.

of the Holy Sepulchre; and there St. Francis stayed for several days in a hermitage above the town.[34]

With its caves, stone steps, grottoes, and ascending paths, Mount La Verna, situated on the eastern border of Tuscany overlooking the Ravenna plain, rises preeminently to the approximate height of Mt. Vesuvius in the region of the Italian Camaldolese hermits who, like the Vallombrosan hermits outside Florence, were influenced by the eremitical practices of the Sinai and Egyptian desert fathers.[35] In the tenth and eleventh centuries, Greek anchorites from Mt. Sinai and the surrounding desert had come to Italy and Sicily and stimulated the Italian Camaldolese movement, a movement dating in tradition from the fourth century when St. Athanasius visited Rome and addressed his *Life of St. Anthony* to Western anchorites. In the 1290s the Mt. Sinai and La Verna eremitical traditions were further joined. As J. P. Migne records, the Franciscan Friar Angelo de Cingulo, employing Latin renderings by "Ambrosio" of the Camaldolese, produced at that time, presumably for the use of monks and pilgrims, the *Scala Paradisi*, a Latin translation of Sinai Bishop John Climacus's seventh-century work the *Heavenly Ladder* (Κλίμαξ θείας ἀγόδου).[36] Climacus's book of thirty meditative steps to God, representing the traditional thirty years of Christ's life before baptism, was to a large degree inspired, as exempla in the text confirm, by the spiritual experiences of anchorites on Mt. Sinai's ladder to God. Over three thousand stone steps, two stone gates, and numerous pilgrimage

---

[34] Paul Sabatier, *Life of St. Francis of Assisi*, trans. Louise Houghton (New York, 1894), pp. 234–300. Sabatier includes a useful critical study of primary sources, 347–432. P. Girolamo Golubovich, *Biblioteca Bio-Bibliografica della Terra Santa e dell' Oriente Francescano* (Firenze, 1906) 1; 1–7, contains historical records on St. Francis's period in Egypt and the Holy Land.

[35] An account of the history of the La Verna area, of the holy shrines and stations of the "Pellegrino alla Verna," and of the medieval "scala" ascended by pilgrims on the mountain La Verna, appears in Piero Bargellini and Vittorio Vettori, *Amoroso viaggio in terra francescana* (Firenzi, 1949). The Camaldolese eremitical movement and establishments are reviewed on pp. 34–45. See also Johannes Jorgensen, *Pilgrim Walks in Franciscan Italy* (London and Edinburgh, 1908), 171–176.

[36] *Patrologiae Cursus Completus*, Series Graeca, ed. J. P. Migne (Paris, 1860), 88: 582. The Latin translation of the *Scala Paradisi* appears in 88: 581–1210. In the *Scala Paradisi*, John Climacus's thirty meditative steps to God are illustrated with stories of virtue from the lives of the "angelic" desert fathers. Step seven includes an account of the Mt. Sinai cell and holy activities of St. Stephanos, the sixth-century monk who gained legendary fame as the Warder of Mt. Sinai's stone Gate of Confession built astride the ascending stone steps on the mountain.

Greek and Latin manuscripts of Climacus's *Scala Paradisi*, often with illuminations showing pilgrims in postures of penitence or climbing a ladder, circulated in Europe in Dante's period. See, for example, John J. Tikken's review of the eleventh or twelfth century Vatican illuminated manuscript copy in "Eine illustrierte Klimax-Handschrift der Vatikanischen Bibliothek," *Acta Societatis Scientiarum Fennicae* 19, no. 2 (1893): 3–16; M. Heppell's study of more than thirty manuscript copies in Slavic monasteries in "Some Slavonic Manuscripts of 'Scala Paradisi,' " *Byzantinoslavica* 18, no. 2 (1957): 233–270; and John Rupert Martin's published collection of ladder illustrations from Greek and Latin sources in *The Illustration of the Heavenly Ladder of John Climacus* (Princeton, 1954). Martin confirms that the Latin translation of the work appeared "at least as early as the thirteenth century" (p. 6). Climacus and Bonaventura were apparently associated as meditative writers, moreover, in the late Italian translation *Santo Iouanni Climacho Altrimenti Scala paradisi* (Venezia, 1492), for the small Pietàs illustrating leaf 2b had previously appeared in an edition of the works of Bonaventura.

"stations," all established by at least the sixth century, enabled medieval pilgrims and monks to move upward from St. Catherine's Monastery at the base to the mountain's summit. To encourage comparable pilgrimage up the pathways and steps of Italian Mount La Verna to sites made holy by St. Francis, the Italian Franciscans in the mid-thirteenth century established various "stations" on the mountain, built the main church La Chiesina, and constructed in 1263 the Stigmata Chapel over the craggy, ribbed rock on which the saint was scored with the wounds of Christ.[37] To foster long Holy Land pilgrimages over the route followed by St. Francis, they founded in the early and mid-thirteenth century, and staffed with Italian clerics, a chain of at least nine pilgrim hospices in the Holy Land that were operating in Dante's period.[38]

Dante in the *Paradiso* precisely identifies that "harsh rock between Tiber and Arno" (XI, 106: "crudo sasso intra Tevero e Arno") on which "serafico" St. Francis received the Stigmata, "l'ultimo sigillo," after returning from the Near East to gather spiritual "fruit from Italian herbage" (XI, 105: "frutto de l'italica erba"). The poet thus alludes, possibly as one who had actually climbed to and seen the rough rock in the Stigmata Chapel, to an Italian pilgrimage site and mountain that had become associated, in part through St. Francis, with Mt. Sion and, through figural and historical relations, with Mt. Sinai and Mt. Tabor. In the circle of the sun of *Paradiso*, moreover, Dante as a pilgrim beyond life sees the blazing form of Illuminato (*Par.* XII, 130), that follower of St. Francis who accompanied the saint from

---

[37] The Chapel of the Stigmata is discussed by Bargelli and Vettori, *Amoroso viaggio*, 21–22; and Jorgensen, *Pilgrim Walks*, 171–176.

[38] P. Girolamo Golubovich in *Biblioteca Bio-Bibliografica della Terra Santa e dell' Oriente Francescano*, vol. 2 (Firenze, 1913) cites records showing that the Franciscans established houses in Egypt and the Holy Land at Damietta, 1220; Jerusalem, 1230; Jaffa, 1252; and Acre, 1217; and he provides evidence of the approximate dates for the establishment of other Franciscan houses at Nicosia, ca. 1252; Aleppo, ca. 1251; Sidon, ca. 1253; Tripoli, ca. 1255; and Tyre, ca. 1255–1256. Further information on the considerable chain of Franciscan houses in the Holy Land, a chain staffed almost exclusively by clerics from Italy and serving pilgrims, has been published in Martiniano Roncaglia, *Storia della Provincia di Terra Santa* (Cairo, 1954), 1: 34–63; and P. Agustin Arce, *Miscelanea de Tierra Santa* (Jerusalem, 1974), 3: 77–81. Fr. Sabino de Sandoli in *Il Primo Convento Francescano in Gerusalemme: 1230-1244* (Jerusalem, 1983), 1–33, maintains that the first Franciscan house in Jerusalem opened in 1217 near what is now the third Station of the Cross on the Via Dolorosa. Golubovich in *Serie Cronologica dei Reverendissimi Superiori di Terra Santa* (Jerusalem, 1898), 3–11, lists the Italian Franciscans, a number of them from Tuscany, who in Dante's period served as the reverend superiors of the Holy Land: Benedetto di Arezzo, ca. 1246; Enrico da Pisa, 1247–1265; Giacamo da Puy, 1266–1269; Andrea da Bologna, ca. 1270; Bartolomeo da Siena, 1278; Giovannino de Parma, no dates; Matteo, 1282; Geleberto, 1286; Giordano, 1306; Guido, 1306; Bonaventura, 1310; Nicolo, 1328; and Frederico da Monte-Vico, 1329.

Paolo Revelli in *L'Italia e il Mar di Levante* (Milano, 1917), provides an informative and most revealing analysis of the strong commercial and cultural associations between Italian and Near Eastern cities in the thirteenth and fourteenth centuries, associations studied in his review of the Eastern Mediterranean outposts and colonies of Rome (pp. 32–50), Venice (pp. 66–78), Genoa (pp. 79–97), and other Italian cities. Revelli discloses some thirty-one Italian colonies or establishments, some of considerable size, in the Eastern Mediterranean in the fourteenth century.

Egypt to the Holy Land. Presenting St. Francis, after Beatrice, as a type of
Christ, Dante in this circle learns from Thomas Aquinas that the saint of
the Stigmata was born on that slope from which there rose into the world
"a sun, even as ours at times rises from the Ganges" (*Par.* XI, 50–51: "un
sole,/ come fa questo talvolta di Gange"); that is, due East from Jerusalem
on medieval T-and-O world iconographic maps. The place of St. Francis's
birth, Aquinas continues, should be called, not Assisi, but "Oriente" (*Par.*
XI, 54).

In the thirteenth and fourteenth centuries before the Protestant Reformation, the veneration of earthly relics and of blessed earthly "stations,"
mountains, temples, and cities was an accepted part of religious practice
in the West. Most substantial forms, as Virgil states in *Purgatorio* XVIII,
were believed to be in union with matter. More important, the spirit had
been made flesh. Icons of the Incarnate Christ of this physical world often
dominated the tympanums and altars of the new Gothic cathedrals, just
as references to the Incarnate Christ frequently dominated the typological
commentary of the period.[39] True imitation in poetry, architecture, or pilgrimage consisted, of course, not in representational invention or action
primarily replicating the accidental forms of matter, but in a conformity of
the immaterial intellect with the immaterial substantial forms underlying
the veil of matter, and in a revelation of those immaterial forms through
personal action or through the "making" of some object or structure. But
in this mortal world most substantial forms were necessarily disclosed
through the instrumentality of matter.

While abstract meditation with the aid of grace was a paramount means
to "true spiritual illumination," medieval meditations usually included the
recollection of holy places and events employing remembered visual images;
and the religious practices of the period made obligatory the acting out of
events through liturgical ritual culminating in the reception of the sacraments.[40] Local or long pilgrimage involving veneration, worship, and re-

---

[39] Georges Duby in *The Age of the Cathedrals,* for example, rightly records that, beginning
in the eleventh century and extending through the centuries of cathedral-building, the "humanity of the Son of God" became the "pivotal point" of a "new" Christian religion, and
that icons of the crucified Christ and relics of the Passion were then prominently placed in
medieval cathedrals (pp. 86–107). See also Johan Chydenius, *The Typological Problem,* pp.
85–98, for remarks on typological commentary of the period stressing the earthly Jerusalem
and the humanity of the Son.

[40] In an idealistic philosophic interpretation of history propounding views which still influence
Dante criticism, G. W. F. Hegel in *The Philosophy of History,* rev. ed., trans. J. Sibree (New
York, 1900) launched in the 1830s a famed attack upon what he regarded as "externals"
devoid of spiritual essences—medieval relics, pilgrimage sites and activities, and other medieval
manifestations of "mundane existence" (p. 391)—and so established an intellectual "climate"
for abstract individualized analyses of even the medieval literal "historical" sense of biblical
events and places.

Hegel objects to the medieval union of the spiritual with the concrete. He praises "looking
for the specific embodiment of Deity," not in a material "earthly sepulchre of stone," but
"rather in the deeper abyss of Absolute Ideality" in a realm of abstraction divorced from
matter (pp. 414, 420). Hegel properly castigates the barbarism of the crusades and the nom-

ception of the sacraments was both a source for and an extension of that ritual. Even the eremitical Camaldolese did more than engage abstractly in the spiritually demanding "steps" of meditation outlined in works such as St. Bonaventura's *Itinerarium mentis in Deum* (ca. 1259) or St. Bernard's *De Gradibus Humilitatis* (ca. 1121), tracts related through monastic and pilgrimage tradition to John Climacus's *Scala Paradisi* and consequently to the stone pilgrimage steps of Mt. Sinai. Some form of figured action, physical as well as spiritual, was required. A religious ritual was physically performed, or the pilgrim's staff was in effect physically grasped, and a fore-

---

inalism of those crusaders and pilgrims obsessed with the grossly physical. But in failing to take into account complex medieval scholastic conceptions of the union of accidents of matter with immaterial substantial forms, and in directing a fierce assault upon the medieval identification of the divine with specific "historical" places and events, he advances positions at variance with medieval belief that a literal, concrete, historical base is necessary for the revelation of spiritual senses in biblical and theological interpretation.

Hegel thus takes exception to that medieval religious faith grounded in part upon the historicity of "mere finite things—. . . the belief that such or such a person existed and said this or that; or that the Children of Israel passed dry-shod through the Red Sea—or that the trumpets before the walls of Jericho produced as powerful an impression as our cannons" (p. 415). He accordingly proclaims, in a radical break with the medieval notion of the literal historical sense of theological allegory, that "all relations that sprang from that vitiating element of externality which we examined above, are *ipso facto* abrogated" (p. 416).

Hegel then replaces concrete medieval historical typology with abstract historical dialectical ideology. Just as foreshadowing types are realized in fulfilled anti-types in medieval figural history, so in Hegel's "Universal history" abstract "consciousness of Freedom on the part of Spirit" is said to lead to "the consequent realization of that Freedom. This development implies a gradation—a series of increasingly adequate expressions or manifestations of Freedom, which result from its Idea." Remarking upon "the *dialectical* nature of the Idea in general," Hegel notes "that it assumes successive forms which it successively transcends" (p. 63).

Hegel's critical comments on Dante in *Aesthetics: Lectures on Fine Art,* trans. T. M. Know, 2 vols. (Oxford, 1975) are, of course, colored by his philosophic posture. In maintaining that a "chief interest" of poetry consists in revealing idealistic, abstract "*universal* doctrines" that "shall be known and believed as universal truth," Hegel argues that in poetry "concrete representation must remain subordinate and indeed external to the content, and allegory is the form which satisfies this need in the easiest and most appropriate way. In this sense Dante has much that is allegorical in his *Divine Comedy.* So there, e.g., theology appears fused with the picture of his beloved Beatrice." Hegel insists that Dante "put into the chief work of his life" very little of the mundane and external, but rather the "inner subjective religion of his heart" (1: 402). Overlooking the social content particularly of *Paradiso,* Hegel contends that in the poem the individual is "an infinite end in himself. . . . In this divine world, concern is purely for the individual" (2: 980). But Hegel as a critic, while imposing a philosophic idealism upon Dante's medieval theological allegory, perceived that in some respects the other world of the work pointed back to events in the earthly world, "The poem comprises the entirety of objective life: the eternal condition of Hell, Purgatory, and Paradise; and on this indestructible foundation the figures of the real world move in their particular character, or rather they *have* moved and now in their being and action are frozen and are eternal themselves in the arms of eternal justice" (2: 1104).

It should be added that Hegel's criticism, though exposing Dante's true spiritual inwardness, nevertheless exaggerates the poet's individual subjectivism. For Dante, as he presents himself in the *Commedia,* is not autonomous. During the poet's processional education through a wondrous love of Beatrice and under the primary guidance of her eyes, Dante's increasingly holy movements of *body,* mind, and soul unquestionably reveal, not a turn from external form, but rather a full and extraordinary merging of external form with spiritual inwardness. Dante's "freedom" is in his conformity to that divine love which he depicts as giving underlying hierarchical order by means of natural law to society and to the entire universe.

shadowing, concrete, historical biblical event was re-enacted and fulfilled in the concrete, historical life of an individual.

HISTORICAL PILGRIMAGE "FULFILLED": EXODUS, REDEMPTION, AND TRANSFIGURATION

Important directional references to Dante's own "historical" twofold pilgrimage to vision in the *Commedia* are introduced during the poet's acted-out Redemption in Eden and beginning spiritual Transfiguration at the outermost edge of the physical universe. At the summit of Mt. Purgatory, Dante imitates scriptural events before a procession signifying the Bible and the Church Militant; and at the summit of the physical universe, before earthly pilgrimage paths and the city of Rome visible in the Book of the World below.

The Book of God's Words—represented by holy Elders and a strange beast, the griffin, signifying Christ—is included among the personages accompanying Beatrice into the Earthly Paradise when she re-encounters Dante mid-way in his pilgrimage beyond life. The Elders, turning to Beatrice who rides in a chariot drawn by the griffin, sing, among other things, "Come to me from Lebanon, my spouse" (*Purg.* XXX, 11: "*Veni, sponsa, de Libano*"), a biblical passage traditionally referring to the marriage of Christ to His Church. "Blessed is he that comes" (*Purg.* XXX, 19: "*Benedictus qui venis!*"), the procession members later cry, words quoted in all four gospels as being called out by the multitude when Christ entered the temple area of Jerusalem. And before Beatrice speaks, nearby angels in the Earthly Paradise establish the Redemptive nature of Dante's actions in the garden by singing the first part of the thirtieth psalm, "*In te, Domine, speravi*" (*Purg.* XXX, 83), which includes the words,

> In manus tuas commendo spiritum meum;
> redemisti me, Domine, Deus veritatis

> Into your hands I commend my spirit, you
> have redeemed me, O Lord, O faithful God

Then Beatrice for the first and only time in the *Commedia* calls the poet by his name, "Dante," and refers to his "vita nuova" (*Purg.* XXX, 55, 115). She next strives to bring the poet's mind and memory to a realization of the direct but lost spiritual pathway to God that had once been open, a pathway that in the new life was such that "every good talent would have made wondrous increase in him" (*Purg.* XXX, 116–117: "ogni abito destro/ fatto averebbe in lui mirabil prova"). It was, of course, Dante's sigh that was described in the sonnet "Oltre la spera" in the *Vita Nuova* as ascending to Beatrice in fulfillment of the prefiguring pilgrimage of Romers. And Beatrice here calls this lost spiritual pathway to mind by referring to the surrounding angels in Eden as the powers controlling the "operations of the mighty spheres that direct each seed to some end, according as the stars are its companions" (*Purg.* XXX, 109–111: "ovra de le rote magne,/

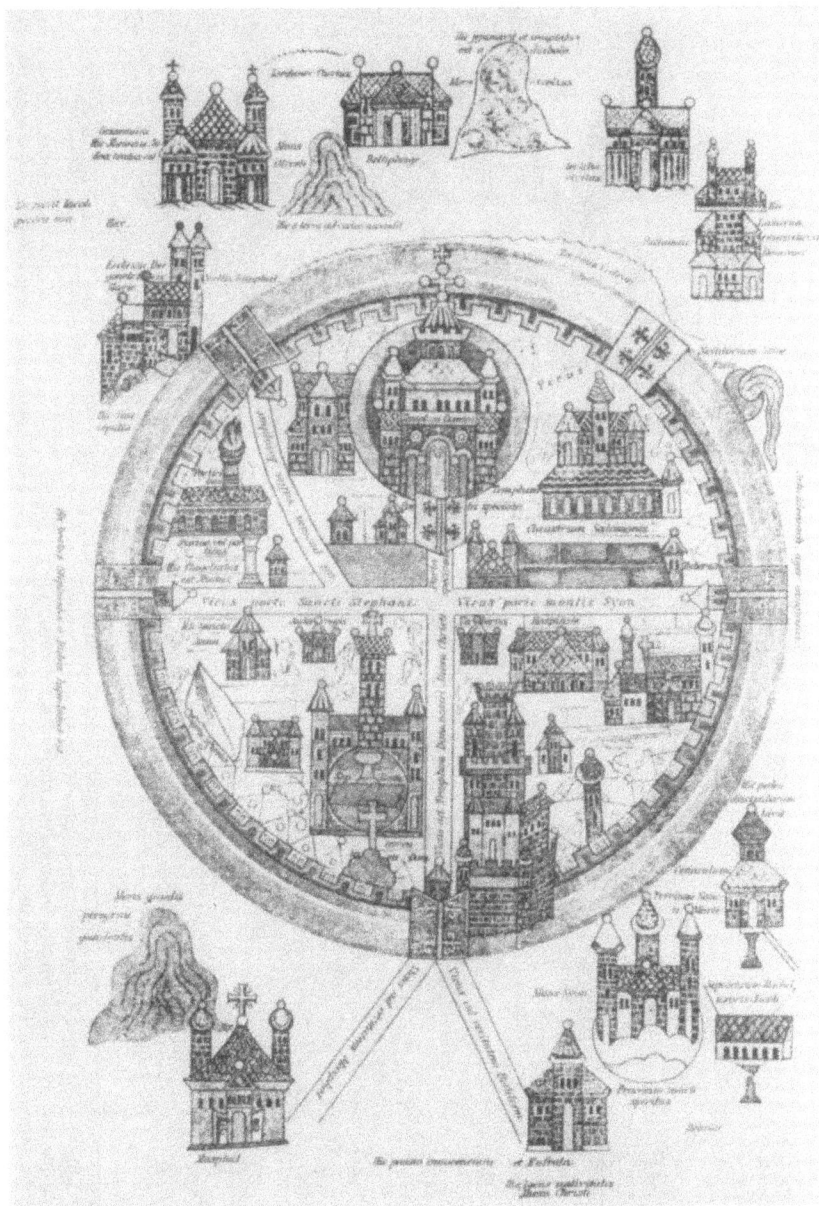

FIG. 5. In consonance with the accounts of pilgrims, the famed medieval cross of Redemption on Golgotha, and the round urn-shaped stone marking the center of the world within the Holy Sepulchre, are reproduced on this map (ca. 1180) from *Itinera Hierosolymitana Crucesignatorum*. The major streets of Jerusalem in themselves form a cross within the perfect circle of the city.

che drizzan ciascun seme ad alcun fine,/ secondo che le stelle son compagne"). Remarking that "he did turn his steps by a way not true" (*Purg.* XXX, 130: "volse i passi suoi per via non vera"), Beatrice then recapitulates,

FIG. 7. Beyond the candelabrum in the foreground, the urn-shaped stone at the medieval center of the world as it stands today in the choir of the Holy Sepulchre, Jerusalem.

FIG. 6. In the apse of St. Pudenziana, Rome, late fourth or early fifth-century Byzantine mosaics depict Christ and the Apostles before actual medieval pilgrimage "stations" of the Redemption in Jerusalem. The earthly Jerusalem here serves as a foreshadowing type for a fulfilled immortal realm. At the left is the round Anastasis of the Holy Sepulchre; at the center, the huge jeweled cross, regularly reproduced on medieval maps of the Holy City, that was erected on Golgotha in the fourth century by Emperor Theodosius I.

34

not the direct journey of the sigh, but the poet's long other-worldly journey to Eden ending with the demand that Dante, in what is clearly a final act in the conversion of his soul, show "pentimento" or penitence (*Purg.* XXX, 145). After Dante confesses his sins and is drawn through the spiritually cleansing waters of Eden's River of Lethe, he experiences a Redeeming vision of Beatrice and is said to taste of that "food which satisfying of itself, causes hunger of itself" (*Purg.* XXXI, 128–129: "cibo/che, saziando di sé, di sé asseta").

Only after presenting visions of the history of Church and empire does Beatrice, repeating the description of the Palmers given in Chapter XIL of the *Vita Nuova*, associate the poet's completed pilgrimage to Eden beyond life with the completed pilgrimage of Palmers to Jerusalem on earth. She insists that Dante remember all that he has seen and heard "for the reason that the pilgrim's staff is brought back wreathed with palm" (*Purg.* XXXIII, 77–78: "che 'l te ne porti dentro a te per quello/che si reca il bordon di palma cinto").

In receiving a type of Christ among character-types signifying the Bible and the Church Militant in Eden beyond life, Dante has fulfilled the foreshadowing actions of a Palmer on earth who, in possession of the truths of the Bible, experiences a conversion of the soul on Exodus pilgrimage pathways and then, moving on to pilgrimage "stations" in Jerusalem, re-enacts the Redemption by receiving Christ as the Eucharist at a "temple" in the Holy City.[41] The poet's actions in Eden are prefigured too, by means of more immediate "home-city" typology pointing to long pilgrimage, in the acted-out Exodus conversion of a pilgrim on the earthly nave floor of a medieval pilgrimage church; and the acted-out Redemption of that pilgrim before a clerical procession, within view of wheel-rose windows or mosaics and paintings of Old and New Testament personages; and finally through that pilgrim's reception of the Eucharist at a central "Jerusalem temple" altar. In the context of Dante's poem, the prefigured and fulfilled events take place during the Easter Season of the Jubilee Pilgrimage year 1300.[42]

---

[41] For discussions of Dante's knowledge of the Jerusalem "temple" and of the poet's figural allusions to the "temple" in the Eden passages, see Robert L. John, *Dante* (Vienna, 1946), 174–181; and *Dante and Michelangelo: Das Paradiso Terrestre und die Sixtinische Decke* (Koln, 1959), 18–21, 45–71; Demaray, *The Invention of Dante's Commedia*, 119–123, 169–174; Rene Guenon, *L'Esoterisme de Dante*, 3rd ed. (Paris, 1949), 9–22; Helmut Hatzfeld, "Modern Literary Scholarship as Reflected in Dante Criticism," *American Critical Essays on The Divine Comedy*, ed. Robert J. Clements (New York and London, 1967), 206–207; and William Anderson, *Dante the Maker*, 277–280, 344–345, 367–370.

An earlier allusion in *Purg.* XV points forward to the appearance of Beatrice, a type of Christ, in an other-worldly location figuring the Old Temple. On the terrace of the wrathful, Dante dreams of the Virgin Mary as she looks for but cannot yet find Christ in the "tempio" (1. 87), the Virgin and her actions serving as an exemplum of that gentleness that is the opposite of wrath.

[42] Anderson in *Dante the Maker* rightly observes that Beatrice's descent to Eden at the core of a holy procession is "remarkably like the splendid peregrinations performed in the cathedrals and great churches of the Gothic period, especially during Lent and Easter" (p. 370). Other critics have found that Dante's meeting with Beatrice and her procession suggest an earthly

Beatrice in Eden also enlarges upon the opening statements of Virgil and Dante in the *Inferno* about the direction of journeys to the heavenly city and to earthly Rome (I, 128; II, 13–33). She now announces with increased figural lucidity Dante's final heavenly and earthly goal: citizenship with her forever in an eternal kingdom, a realm identified with Christ and with Rome. "You shall be with me forever," Beatrice declares, "a citizen of that Rome whereof Christ is a Roman" (*Purg.* XXXII, 101–102: "sarai meco sanza fine cive/di quella Roma onde Cristo è romano").

Dante, however, is consistently behind in his grasp of his position as a pilgrim; and Beatrice in the Earthly Paradise declares that his mind has turned to "pietra" or stone (*Purg.* XXXIII, 74).[43] Yet when the poet in *Paradiso*

---

encounter with clerics bearing Christ in the form of the Host; see Lizette Andrews Fisher, *The Mystic Vision*, 102–116; and Bernard Stambler, *Dante's Other World* (New York, 1957), 27–35. Johan Chydenius in *The Typological Problem*, 70–73, gives an example of how the church of Santa Croce in Gerusalemme, Rome, served in the literal sense as an anti-type for the earthly Jerusalem as manifest in the earliest preserved epistolary: the seventh-century *Comes* of John of Wurzburg. "The texts for the stational mass," Chydenius writes, "which was said *ad Hierusalem* on the fourth Sunday in Lent were specially selected to be appropriate for this locality." He adds that "in the mass in question, the idea of pilgrimage to Jerusalem is prominent to the end" (pp. 71–72). Margaret R. Miles in "The Fourth Century: Architecture, Images, and Liturgy," *Images as Insight: Visual Understanding in Western Christianity and Secular Culture* (Boston, 1985), more widely traces the correlation between early Roman liturgy and church processional architecture, noting that "Christian liturgy was markedly-peripatetic" (p. 52). See also Jeffrey T. Schnapp's *The Transfiguration of History at the Center of Dante's Paradise* (Princeton, 1986), 170–238, for readings of Transfiguration and church typology in *Paradiso* XIV–XVIII. Schnapp, studying what he terms Dante's "poetics of martyrdom," finds the apsidal mosaics of the Transfiguration in the Byzantine church of St. Apollinare in Classe, Ravenna, to be reflected in their general typal outlines in the Transfiguration iconography of Dante's sphere of Mars.

[43] Giuseppe Mazzotta in his chapter "Allegory" in *Dante: Poet of the Desert* (Princeton, 1979), 227–274, discusses Dante's limitations and failures of memory, the poet's images of "scattering" and closure, and the poet's constant admissions that poetic depiction falls short of reality. Mazzotta, on the basis of his own critical analysis, then accepts Eric Auerbach's "hesitant conclusion that Dante disrupts the order he creates" (p. 270). But by not exploring the earthly and heavenly figural "inversions" that sustain even as they re-order typological relations, and by leaning in his independent criticism away from the progressions of medieval "historical" typological allegory and toward the assumed "contradictions" of Hegelian abstract dialectic, Mazzotta advances an extreme case for the fragmentation of Dante's verse in suggesting the possibility of a "double reading of the poem. The *Divine Comedy*," he writes, "overtly tells the story of the pilgrim's progress from the sinful state of the 'selva oscura' to beatific vision of *Paradise* XXXIII. . . . It also tells the story of persistent ambiguity of metaphoric language in which everything is perpetually fragmented and irreducible to any unification" (p. 269). These two possible "opposed readings," he urges, "do not deconstruct and cancel each other out, but are simultaneously present and always involve each other" (p. 270). Dante's text for *Paradiso* XXXIII and elsewhere "actually, originates from the confusions and fragmentations of a blotted memory, the only trace of which," Mazzotta adds in a phrase echoing the subjectivism of Hegel, "is the impression of sweetness in the heart" (p. 265).

Ambiguities in the metaphoric language of medieval vision, of a kind reviewed from a scholastic hierarchical perspective by Jacques Maritain in *The Degrees of Knowledge*, trans. under Gerald B. Phelan from the fourth French edition (New York, 1959), are indeed pervasive in the *Commedia*. These ambiguities are particularly noticeable in *Paradiso*, for there Dante is constantly transcending his slowly-acquired awareness of earthly centers below even as, having turned from pilgrimage goals on earth to heaven, his powers are only partially capable of understanding paradisal centers above. But through an encompassing language giving expression to Dante's imitative and often "inverted" figural actions and associated experiences, an essentially harmonious, hierarchical pattern of linguistic meanings emerges throughout the

ascends to the realm of the stars, when from this spiritual and physical perspective he looks down upon true and false pilgrimage routes upon earth, he is directly confronted with certain literal "truths" about the first

---

text. The poem as an unfolding structure of words allows for the connatural aesthetic illumination of the reader if not, in every case, of Dante himself.

The critical argument for Dante's alleged reaction against a hierarchical cosmos, through delineation of the heretics Farinata degli Uberti and the elder Cavalcante (*Inf. X,* 31–130), was put forward by Erich Auerbach in *Mimesis: The Representation of Reality in Western Literature,* trans. Willard Trask (Princeton, 1953), 174–202, and is quoted by Mazzotta in *Dante: Poet of the Desert,* 231–232.

"By virtue of this immediate and admiring sympathy with man," writes Auerbach, "the principle, rooted in the divine order, of the indestructibility of the whole historical and individual man turns *against* that order, makes it subservient to its own purposes, and obscures it. The image of man eclipses the image of God. Dante's work made man's Christian-figural being a reality, and destroyed it in the very process of realizing it" (p. 202).

Basing this conclusion on Dante's extraordinary power and poetic virtuosity in depicting the human, earthly passions and thoughts of the two heretics, Auerbach, under the influence of the Reformation views and philosophical dialectic of Hegel who is cited, says of the contemptuous, caustic, and arrogant Farinata who rises from a burning tomb: "We cannot but admire Farinata" (p. 200). Weeping Cavalcante, whose head alone at first appears above the tomb, asks questions about his son on earth; and so is surprisingly found by Auerbach to exhibit a "belief in the autonomous greatness of the human mind" (p. 172). Thus Auerbach restates a Hegelian argument in claiming that Dante, by means of character representation, "opened the way for that aspiration toward autonomy which possesses all earthly existence" (p. 200); and "we" are said to wish to "weep with Cavalcante" (p. 200).

Human sympathy, at least for Cavalcante, is indeed elicited by the representation. But the difficulty with Auerbach's aesthetic-ideological critique is that it reflects a nineteenth-century Hegelian outlook but makes no mention of medieval Averroism, a central theme of the episode and one of the abiding explicit and implicit themes in Dante's *Commedia.* Through the *contrapasso* actions and speeches of the excessively arrogant Farinata and the excessively helpless Cavalcante, the poet by means of event and radically individualized characters presents an aesthetically effective satire of heretics dedicated to Averroistic doctrines, doctrines attacked and in some measure unveiled in St. Thomas Aquinas's *De Unitate Intellectus Contra Averroistas* (ca. 1270), trans. Beatrice H. Zedler (Milwaukee, 1968). St. Thomas, organizing his treatise under two main topics, first offers a rebuttal to the Averroistic contention that the intellect is separate from the body, a view that Dante bluntly mocks by having Farinata rise in body and mind from an infernal tomb. Next, St. Thomas takes issue with the Averroistic doctrine that there is for all persons one universal intellect that apprehends in the present universal ideas, a doctrine that Dante stunningly satirizes by creating heretics having highly individualized knowledge of the past and future, but lacking and yet desiring highly individualized knowledge of the present.

Dante's characterizations are unforgettable. But given the prominance of Averroism as a heresy in the poet's period, educated medieval readers would, it seems to me, have considered the Farinata-Cavalcante scene as embodying, not a refutation of traditional hierarchical scholastic views of the person and the universe, but rather a defense of those views.

Anthony K. Cassell in *Dante's Fearful Art of Justice* (Toronto and Buffalo, 1984) has recently urged that the "stance of both Farinata and Cavalcante, once the latter too rises to full height," is the figural antithesis of "a new Gothic vision of a naked Christ," a vision captured beginning in the twelfth century in icons and art works showing Christ standing " 'waist-up,' alone and unsupported in his sarcophagus." Noting that Emile Mâle believed the prototype for this new devotional image to be the twelfth-century mosaic icon of the Passion in the Church of Santa Croce in Gerusalemme, Rome, Cassell points out that the Santa Croce mosaic "commanded particular veneration as a pilgrim station especially on Passion Sunday and Good Friday." Cassell records that the subject matter and provenance of the mosaic are in dispute, but he maintains that "there are certainly enough examples of the 'Imago pietatis' dating close to Dante's time and experience to prove the Poet's most intimate familiarity with it." He writes of the Santa Croce mosaic, however, that "if Mâle's thesis were right, we could be sure that Dante viewed it on his Roman pilgrimage during the Jubilee Year of 1300" (pp. 24–25).

FIG. 8. The Greek Orthodox altar in the Holy Sepulchre at the traditional site of the cross, a cross proclaimed in medieval pilgrimage texts to have been made from the tree of life that grew in Eden. A glass-covered aperture in the altar permits a view of the cleft rock through which, according to medieval pilgrimage tradition, the blood of the second Adam flowed down upon the entombed skull of the first Adam.

In Dante's Eden voices murmur the name "Adamo" just before a cross is formed by the juncture of a spar of Beatrice's chariot and the tree of life.

stage of his twofold earthly and other-worldly long pilgrimage. These are the "truths" that Beatrice in Eden sought without success to convey by mentioning the "vita nuova" and by pressing the poet to recall alternate short and long pilgrimage pathways on earth and beyond life first revealed in the earlier work. Dante amid the stars is now in a position to understand

Fig. 9. At the medieval "New Jerusalem" of San Stefano, Bologna, an urn-shaped stone, replicating the one at the world's center in Jerusalem, stands before an Italian figural reconstruction of the temple of the Holy Sepulchre. From the tenth through the twelfth centuries, a chain of pilgrimage "stations," fulfilled types of those in the Holy City, were established at San Stefano so that persons could re-enact a Jerusalem pilgrimage while remaining at home.

Fig. 10. A fountain of the familiar Near Eastern urn configuration before the "circular" holy structure—actually the seventh-century Dome-of-the-Rock Sanctuary (Kubbet-es-Sakhra)—that many medieval pilgrims believed to be the Temple of Solomon. The "temple's" supposed dimensions, as recorded in the Bible, served in theory and on occasion in fact as a model for the numerological figurism of European and British churches.

in retrospect, and even more completely to fulfill, what Beatrice in Eden suggested and what events in the garden confirmed. Speaking to Dante in a fashion that embraces the "historical" literal sense of an allegory of the theologians, Beatrice unmistakably declares before the Apostle St. James that

> "La Chiesa militante alcun figliuolo
>   non ha con più speranza com' è scritto
>   nel Sol che raggia tutto nostro stuolo:
> però li è conceduto che d'Egitto
>   vegna in Jerusalemme per vedere,
>   anzi che 'l militar li sia prescritto."

(Par. XXV, 52–57)

> "Church Militant has not a child richer in hope,
>   as is written in the sun which irradiates all
>   our host,
> therefore was it granted him to come from Egypt
>   to Jerusalem to see, before the term of his
>   warfare is completed."

Through the literal sense of her words, Beatrice clearly says that Dante during his lifetime has come, not from the earthly world to the world beyond life, but from "Egypt" to "Jerusalem." She calls the poet a child, not of the heavenly Church Triumphant, but of the earthly Church Militant. By means of these typological back-references to prefiguring "historical" earthly events, Beatrice authoritatively reminds the poet that, in acting out a twofold "historical" journey, he has made *in figura* the foreshadowing earthly pilgrimage of the Palmers first mentioned in Chapter XLI of the *Vita Nuova*.[44] It is this foreshadowing earthly pilgrimage, in imitation of

---

[44] Using medieval theological, philosophical, and literary works, A. C. Charity in *Events and their Afterlife: The Dialectics of Christian Typology in the Bible and Dante* (Cambridge, England, 1966), convincingly shows how the poet grounded his other-worldly pilgrimage in such an autobiographical "back-reference to a history prior to that directly narrated." Dante's pilgrimage beyond based upon this "back-reference," Charity notes, is adjusted—after the manner of medieval legendary lives of St. Francis, St. Paul, and other holy persons—so as to be interpreted as an imitation of biblical events ultimately focused upon the life of Christ. Citing Fra Bartolomeo's *De Conformitate Vitae B. Francisci ad Vitam Domini Jesu* as an example, Charity writes that "undeniably, a historical basis exists for the most part behind each unit of narrative," but that "the fundamentally theological point in the *imitatio Christi* is brought out by setting event opposite event from the life of the Saviour and servant. In the earlier 'Lives' of St. Francis, stylization of incident and evocative phrase together do the same work." Commentators should "look further back still," Charity urges, to "New Testament narratives" for other examples of how back-references to "historical" episodes help to mold the depiction of holy lives. "There too," Charity remarks, "in St. Paul's journey to Jerusalem, a self conforming with the life of Christ is presented by indirect means, in phraseology and echo." Dante's journey beyond life, Charity adds, "retains still an autobiographic substance with which it never loses contact" through back-references to the true, "literal sense" of the poet's past historical life. He adds that "the figuring, the stylizing, of Dante's life, on this view, remains vital, a necessary means of expressing something he felt about it. It is done for the sake of

ARCHITECTURAL TYPOLOGY AND STRUCTURE   41

the biblical Exodus of Moses and the Israelites, that has been the historical type and the "true" existential base for Dante's fulfilled "historical" journey beyond life from hell, the anti-type for earthly Egypt, to the "milizia" or soldiery of the Church Militant in Eden, the anti-type for earthly Jerusalem (*Purg.* XXXII, 22). Beatrice's remarks carry with them the additional typological suggestion that the poet's other-worldly pilgrimage to Eden, in the manner of other recurrent biblical imitative actions in the poem, in turn foreshadowed and now in some respects is further fulfilled in the poet's

---

making a point of theology, or better, for the sake of a claim made by means of typology. . . . this, Dante may say, is my own self-conforming with Christ" (pp. 253–255).

Although Charity contrasts the historicity of the foreshadowed earthly events with the many mythic qualities implicit in the depiction of fulfilled events beyond life, he stresses too, referring to Auerbach's comments on the historicity of both earthly and other-worldly figurism, that there is a "certain historical dependency and continuity between the events which typology relates" (p. 199). He thus finds, giving attention to the allegorical statements in Letter X, that the fulfilled events beyond life in the *Commedia* embody "typological back-references as well as forward ones," that in the other world "Dante's journey is a type of his future" (pp. 247–249).

William Anderson in *Dante the Maker*, also addressing the question of the importance of Christ's life in history to allegorical interpretation, critically reviews at length "the method of *figura*, a method which depends on the historicity both of the character or event described and the people or happenings with which it is compared, as the strength and sufferings of Samson were regarded as a type of the strength and sufferings of Christ, or as in Dante's journey the Great Circle pilgrimage is a figure of his own travels from the spiritual Jerusalem to the eternal Rome. But this method can easily be related to the allegorical level of the fourfold method, which relates past and present events in the light of the role of Christ's life in the history of the world" (pp. 331–332). For an analysis of the Redemption typology in the Eden section, and of the pervasive fourfold allegorical meanings as they relate to Dante's typology, see also Demaray, particularly the chapter "Three Typological Modes of Dante's *Commedia*: Biblical Imitation, Internal Recurrence, and Worldly Imitation," *The Invention of Dante's Commedia*, pp. 93–115.

Total consistency in Dante's long and complex poem is not to be expected, but a general critical posture toward the work is necessary. By now it should be very clear that exception is here taken to the once-traditional view that the work is primarily an allegory of the poets with a fictional literal sense, a view recently re-stated by Bruno Nardi in *Nel mondo di Dante* (Roma, 1944) and by G. Paparelli in "Fictio: la definizione dantesca della poesia," *Ideologia e poesia di Dante* (Firenzi, 1975), 53–138. Charles Singleton in *Dante Studies I* (Cambridge, Mass., 1954) and *Dante Studies II* (Cambridge, Mass., 1958) has persuasively urged that Dante in the *Commedia* should be considered as writing theological allegory with a "historical" literal sense. Readings of the spiritual senses of Dante's theological allegory have been offered by Robert Hollander in *Allegory in Dante's Commedia* (Princeton, 1969), and Pompeo Giannantonio in *Dante e l'allegorismo* (Firenzi, 1969).

Recent re-interpretations of the poet's allegory often tend to overstate, in my view, genuine themes and elements in Dante's verse. John Freccero in "The Dance of the Stars: Paradiso X," *Dante: The Poetics of Conversion,* ed. Rachel Jacoff (Cambridge, Mass. and London, 1986), 224–225, reprinted from *Dante Studies* 86 (1986): 85–111, calls attention to fictional elements in *Paradiso* in cautiously suggesting that Dante, supposedly using the "technique and terms" of Plato while under the "inspiration" of the Bible, "seems to fashion his representation according to what might be called the allegory of the poets." Freccero notes in particular Beatrice's statement in *Paradiso* IV, 37–63, that the physical appearance of souls in the sphere of the moon, far from their true seats in the Empyrean, is arranged by heaven so that Dante can have appropriate sensible matter from which to abstract intellectually and so to understand. Interpreting this physical appearance as Dante's accommodation of Platonic myth, Freccero too quickly abandons distinctions in claiming that "the structure of the *cantica* depends, not upon a principle of *mimesis*, but rather upon metaphor: the creation of a totally new reality out of elements so disparate as to seem contradictory by any logic other than that of poetry" (222).

ascent to the stars. Here in this stellar realm of the Book of the Cosmos Dante, as a true child of the Church Militant, learns that his hope is "written" in the sun. This blazing orb shines upon what Beatrice declares to be the "hosts of Christ's triumph" (*Par.* XXIII, 19–20: "schiere/del triunfo di Cristo"), that is, the hosts of the Son rather than of the entire Trinity.

The hosts of Christ's Triumph are an unusual and often misinterpreted figural amalgam, representing fully neither the earthly Church Militant seen in the physical world below in the Earthly Paradise, nor the heavenly Church Triumphant later to appear above in the immaterial Empyrean. The hosts are there to exalt the Son of medieval Incarnation theology, a

---

The "reality" of the canto, however, is not "totally new." While the positioning of souls in lower spheres can in part be considered a possible concession by Dante to Platonic myth, it nevertheless again is apparent that in *Paradiso* as elsewhere in the *Commedia* the souls themselves, through Dante's application of a historical and mimetic worldly and biblical typology, continue to fulfill life beyond life their prefiguring earthly reality.

Freccero does not mention that Beatrice states in *Paradiso* IV that these souls in the sphere of the moon are not like—"non è simile"—those discussed by Plato in the *Timaeus*, souls that Plato, according to this lady, falsely says receive their "forma" from Nature in the stars to which they are supposed to return (49–54). Beatrice adds that Plato may possibly be correct only if he means that the influence of the souls is evident in the stars (58–60). By contrast, Beatrice defends the souls' outward physical manifestation in the moon's sphere by an appeal to the authority of the Bible. This lady explains to Dante, as Freccero observes, that the truth of scripture similarly "condescends to your capacity, and attributes hands and feet to God having other meaning" (*Par.* IV, 43–45: "condescende/ e vostra facultate, e piedi e mano/ attribuisce a Dio e altro intende").

Something more than vague biblical "inspiration" is at work here. Freccero chooses to emphasize certain external and adjusted accidental material forms—elements in the sensible veil shrouding transcendent reality—that are in part based upon the poet's possible, tentative accommodation of Platonic myth. Dante mentions the myth but emphasizes the necessity of adjusting accidental material forms to reveal an underlying reality resting upon biblical truth. The poet in theory as well as practice, while introducing mythic elements, thus continues to present souls as figural creations in what is essentially a historical "allegory of the theologians." Dante's "artistic" problem in depicting souls, as moving beings with transformed but physical bodies in changing or changeless realms beyond life, is taken up in my "Three Typological Modes," *The Invention of Dante's Commedia*, 112–115. .

Examining what he regards as Dante's special visionary and yet secularized "theological allegory," Gian Roberto Sorolli in his forcefully argued *Prolegomena alla Divina Commedia* (Firenzi, 1971)—aware of how the other world of the poem points back *in figura* to Empire, Church, and society on earth—strains his interpretation, it seems to me, in transforming Dante the reformer into a kind of divinely-ordained prophetic missionary, and the *Commedia* into a form of fiery prophecy that is assumed to be focused primarily upon issues of earthly world order. And Giuseppe Mazzotta in *Dante: Poet of the Desert*, accepting what is here regarded as Auerbach's misinterpretation of the Farinata episode (see my note 43) and citing the failure during Beatific Vision of some of Dante's faculties, leans too much toward an insistence upon the discontinuity and "fragmentation" of the language and meaning of the *Commedia*.

Taking a modern idealist posture that the "only external referent" upon which Dante based the truth of the *Commedia* is a transcendent God, Teodolinda Barolini in *Dante's Poets: Textuality and Truth in the Commedia* (Princeton, 1984), 90–91, elaborating upon an argument espoused by Mazzotta and not addressing the range of criticism on Dante's mimetic uses of the Bible and the World, advances forms of the authorial autonomy and the poetic discontinuity theories in insisting that Dante, "unchecked" and with "absolute freedom and authority," reassigns new values entirely on his own to the world and to history. "Because none of us can check with God as to what Dante saw, or . . . as to the fidelity of Dante's transcription," writes Barolini of *Purg.* XXIV and *Par.* X on the assumption that God alone, and not the Bible and

Divine-Human Being of flesh and spirit and the Second Person of the Trinity. In this outermost extremity of the physical universe bordering immaterial realms, they appear in the form of stars, those luminously spiritual and yet "mediating" physical objects that direct humanity from the material cosmos to the eternal. The bright central sun, a type for the Human-Divine Christ, is actually said by Beatrice to have a power and might that opens "the pathways between heaven and earth" (*Par.* XXIII, 38: "le strade tra 'l cielo e la terra"). And among the stars, the earthly mother of Christ, the Virgin Mary, appropriately re-enacts her bodily Assumption into heaven, thus illustrating the way from the earthly to the divine and confirming the union of matter and spirit (*Par.* XXIII, 88–120). "There is the Rose," Beatrice says of the Virgin, "wherein the Divine Word made itself flesh" (*Par.* XXIII, 73–74: "Quivi è la rosa in che 'l verbo divino/carne si fece").

The stellar hosts and the blazing sun thus figure forth the fulfilled realm of the Incarnate Christ at the material-spiritual border of the cosmos, a realm that is the transcendent anti-type of some events and personages of the Church Militant in an Eden figuring the Redemption in Jerusalem, and a prefiguring type and partial embodiment of events and personages of the Church Triumphant in the Empyrean figuring the Transfiguration in Rome. Some typological references, viewed retrospectively, point back first to the "milizia" in the Earthly Paradise and then to the Holy City on Mt. Sion; other selective references point forward to the heavenly city of the rose that is the fulfillment of the Italian city of Church and Empire. Yet

---

the World, serves as Dante's only index to truth, "the apparently humble role of scribe results in a license to write the world, in fact to play God unchecked." Barolini provides most subtle and revealing insights into how Dante acts as an original critic and historian of poetry; but in discussing Dante's philosophic-theological attitudes toward universal history, the iconographic Book of the World, and poetic invention, Barolini, by adopting an idealist philosophic perspective, arrives at critical conclusions that, I think, require qualification. "The *Comedy,*" she writes, "respects no truth but its own, least of all that composite and approximate truth men know as history"; and she asserts that the poetic "strategy of the *Comedy* is that there is no strategy."

While fundamentally accepting Singleton's view of the *Commedia* as theological allegory, this writer, nonetheless, cannot agree with Singleton's claim that the earthly action "shadowed" or "reflected" in Dante's other-worldly pilgrimage concerns *only* the abstract, interior spiritual experiences of heart, mind, and soul—the "*itinerarium mentis ad Deum*"—of the reader or wayfarer (See Singleton, especially *Dante Studies II,* 4–12). Rather, experiences of body, heart, mind, and soul can be seen to be encompassed in foreshadowing earthly action that, for critical and historical and theological-philosophical reasons, definitely also needs to be regarded as historically "true." A. C. Charity in *Events and their Afterlife* has properly argued against Singleton's purely "abstract" view of reflected earthly action, observing that the foreshadowing and "historical" earthly "journey is a life lived, not just thought of" (p. 253).

Erich Auerbach, therefore, rightly insisted upon the necessary historicity and continuity of both foreshadowing earthly types and fulfilled other-worldly antitypes. Charity, conscious of Incarnation theology, effectively disclosed that the figurism of Dante's own biblically-ordered journey beyond life refers back to foreshadowing concrete, historical events in the poet's earthly life. And Anderson, equally aware of Incarnation theology, appropriately integrated material and spiritual elements by interpreting the historical types and antitypes of Dante's twofold great circle Egypt-Jerusalem-Rome and other-worldly journey in the light of the spiritual senses of theological allegory and the *itinerarium mentis ad Deum* of meditative tradition.

FIG. 11. The mosaic of the Transfiguration in the apse of St. Vitale, Ravenna.

FIG. 12. The sixth-century mosaic of the Transfiguration in the apse of the Church of the Transfiguration, Mt. Sinai.

the stars in their all-important midway region serve in themselves as spiritual-physical guiding lights, lights to which Dante strikingly alludes by ending each canticle with the word "stelle." It is the dazzling light of the sun, however, that most powerfully guides Dante, and by implication all humanity, from the physical universe into immaterial regions of eternal vision.

In the Earthly Paradise the four nymphs of the cardinal virtues had drawn Dante into their dance singing, "here we are nymphs and in heaven we are stars" (*Purg.* XXXI, 106: "Noi siam qui ninfe e nel ciel siamo stelle"). But the three dancing nymphs of the theological virtues, prefigurations of the three circling Apostles of the Transfiguration in the stellar heavens, had in Eden only moved toward the poet without reaching him (*Purg.* XXXI, 131–132). Now by answering questions posed by the Transfiguration Apostles Peter, James, and John, Dante defines and embraces each of the theological virtues and so takes a final step to spiritual union with the Son. The poet also enters into a period of transfiguring visionary experience when he raises his eyes to the blinding but spiritually illuminating light of the Apostle John (*Par.* XXV, 119). For Dante, in this middle realm of the stars, transcendently confirms his earlier position as a child of the earthly Church Militant, becomes a member of the hosts of the Second Person of the Trinity, and begins his admission to the heavenly Church Triumphant of triune Godhead.

After Dante finally ascends from the stellar sphere to the shore of right love that is the immaterial Primum Mobile, the region where the angels who move the spheres have their "tempio," the poet learns from his lady that twofold directional influences indeed emanate from these realms at the border of the physical and spiritual universe. In the words of Beatrice,

> Questi ordini di sù tutti s'ammirano,
>   e di giù vincon sì, che verso Dio
>   tutti tirati sono e tutti tirano.
>
> (Par. XXVIII, 127–129)

> These orders all gaze upward, and downward
>   have such conquering might that toward God
>   all are drawn and all draw.

The poet in fact has already demonstrated an implied knowledge of the true figural pathway to the Church Triumphant and the Creator. In defining Faith before St. Peter in the sphere of the stars, Dante elaborates upon his earlier assertion in *Inferno* II on the journey of St. Paul. The poet had noted that St. Paul traveled over the general route of Aeneas to the "holy place, where the Successor of the greatest Peter sits" (23–24: "loco santo,/ u' siede il successor del maggior Piero"). Among the stars the poet again alludes to St. Paul, the "dear brother" of St. Peter, and to Rome in stating,

> . . . Come 'l verace stilo
>   ne scrisse, padre, del tuo caro frate
>   che mise teco Roma nel buon filo,
> fede è sustanza di cose sperate
>   e argomento de le non parventi;
>   e questa pare a me sua quiditate.
>
> (Par. XXIV, 61–66)

> . . . As the veracious pen of your dear brother
>   wrote of it, who with you, father, put Rome
>   on the good path,
> Faith is the substance of things hoped for
>   and the evidence of things not seen;
>   and this I take to be its quiddity.

Later when Dante reaches that eternal Church Triumphant of the rose, which is compared to earthly Rome (*Par.* XXXI, 31–36), Beatrice extends allusions both to Florence and to the final stage of twofold Rome-heaven pilgrimage initially recorded in the *Vita Nuova*, XL-XLII. She unequivocally declares what, in the literal sense of Dante's journey beyond to the eternal city of heaven, can only now in context be considered "true": that the poet has traveled to the "divine from the human, to the eternal from time. . . . and from Florence to a people just and sane" (*Par.* XXXI, 37–39: "divino da l'umano,/a l'etterno dal tempo . . . ,/e di Fiorenza in popol giusto e sano"). Beatrice's assertion in its literal sense could not have been made before the hosts of the Christ Triumphant in the material stellar heavens; her pronouncement is reserved for Dante's actual arrival at the celestial rose in the immaterial Empyrean.

From combined allusions in the *Vita Nuova* and the *Commedia*, it can be seen that Dante journeyed from Beatrice's city of Florence, in a realm of time and change, to a hell figuring Egypt, to an Eden figuring Jerusalem, and then to a just and timeless heavenly city figuring Rome. After writing of his journey to the heavenly city, Dante hopes to return, he confesses to St. Peter and Beatrice amid the stars (*Par.* XXV, 4–12), to the font of his baptism in the "fair sheepfold" or "bello ovile" of Florence, there to be crowned poet laureate.[45]

FROM EGYPT TO JERUSALEM: SPIRITUAL CONVERSION ON EARTH AND BEYOND

A cultural gulf separates modern historical consciousness dependent upon empirical "fact" and medieval typological and iconographic con-

---

[45] In *The Political Vision of Dante* (Princeton, 1984), Joan Ferrante, in a thematic reading of political and mercantile references in the *Commedia*, places special emphasis upon the "sixth canto of each cantica" which, she argues, "focuses on the political entity that serves as the model for that cantica: in Hell, it is Florence, in Purgatory, Italy, and in Paradise, the Roman empire" (p. 47). Certain distinctions—rephrased from an earlier article "Florence and Rome, the Two Cities of Man in the *Divine Comedy*," *The Early Renaissance Acta* 5 (1978), pp. 1–9— are used in advancing the case for models. Purgatory is said to be "like Italy" (p. 46). "The Italy evoked in Purgatory is partly the physical entity," she writes, "in that Purgatory is a mountain surrounded by sea; but it is primarily cultural" (p. 47). By contrast, the model for hell is found to be "the physical and historical reality" of just "contemporary Florence," not the Florence of the past or the future (p. 47). She adds that "Paradise is based on an idealized Rome" (p. 47).

Ferrante helpfully points out allusions to the infernal political and social evils of "contemporary Florence" as a mercantile city state, and to Rome as the idealized center for world order and justice. Nevertheless, the assumption that Italian and related political allusions together with mercantile references, however numerous or strongly felt by Dante, fully reveal the all-embracing "models" for other-worldly realms seems to me misleading, particularly in a political-philosophical-theological poem such as the *Commedia*. By not critically engaging the rich commentary on Dante's biblical allegory involving alternative and complementary "models" for the poet's realms beyond life, Ferrante, in my view, limits Dante's meaning.

It should be noted that even corrupt, mercantile Florence is advanced as a model for hell only by means of arguable distinctions resting on the word "contemporary." In the remembered "present" of actions in the *Commedia* that might well be considered "contemporary," Florence despite all of its evils remains the city of the blessed Beatrice's life and death; the "sheepfold" beset by wolves but still "fair" to which Dante wishes to return (*Par.* XXV, 4–9); the city that, as Ernst Robert Curtius discerned, gave up thirty-two of its citizens to Dante's hell, but also four citizens to the poet's purgatory, and two citizens to the poet's paradise. Florence is thus depicted as a place of much evil but also of some exceptional holiness.

Although Dante was powerfully influenced by mercantile matters and by "visionary" and practical politics involving Florence, Italy, and the "Holy Roman Empire," he can be seen to cast political and mercantile elements and types, together with the myriad details of his poem, within the all-embracing figurism of universal Hebraic-Christian history as disclosed with ultimate authority in the Bible and in the iconography of the full World and Cosmic Book of God's Works. The final cantos, not primarily the sixth cantos, of each cantica best reveal the virtuous guides, the "source books," and the figured sites and characters that provide the dominating earthly "models" for realms beyond life.

FIG. 13. The Transfiguration mosaic in the apse of SS. Cosma and Damiano, Rome.

FIG. 14. Sunlight rays down from the East next to the traditional tomb of Christ in the Anastasis ambulatory, Jerusalem. On Easter Sunday morning in medieval times as at present, a priest carried a single flaming candle from the tomb and lighted the candles of nearby celebrants. This Ceremony of the Holy Fire, passed by way of pilgrims to Dante's home city, was imitated in public ceremonies in medieval Florence at Easter.

FIG. 15. Reconstructions of the twelve columns, said by Eusebius in the fourth century to signify the twelve Apostles, still surround the traditional tomb of the Son in the Anastasis of the Holy Sepulchre.

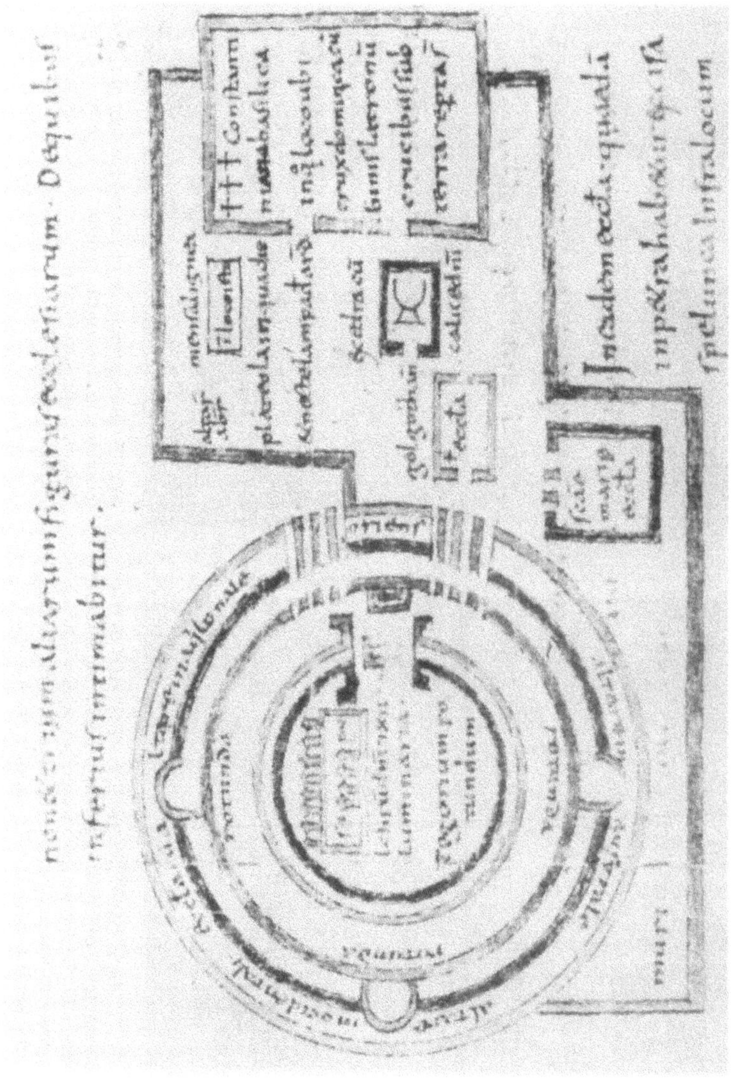

Fig. 16. The earliest detailed ground plan drawing of the Holy Sepulchre. From the Holy Land pilgrimage narrative of Arculf (ca. 670).

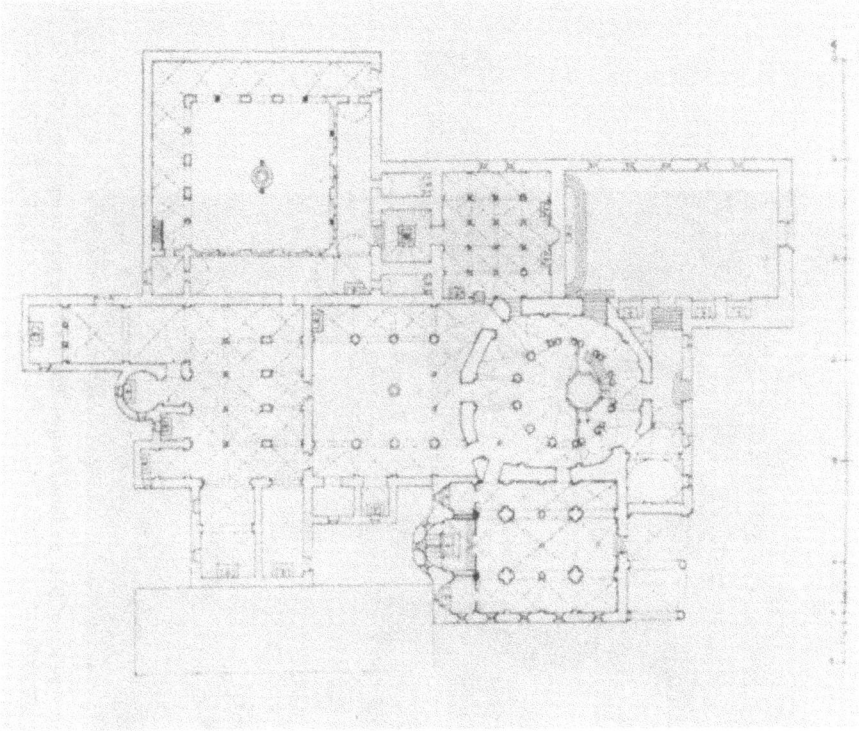

FIG. 17. A modern drawing of the medieval ground plan of the figured Holy Sepulchre at San Stefano, Bologna. A circle of columns, single or paired, form twelve supports about the figured tomb of the Son.

sciousness that, as can be seen in the *Commedia,* molds personal life to a divine figural framework. A central interpretive problem arises from this separation.

Although the *Commedia* is frequently and, in my view, correctly interpreted in general as an allegory of the theologians with a literal sense considered as if historically true, Beatrice's pronouncement about Dante's journey from Egypt to Jerusalem in the poet's lifetime (*Par.* XXV, 52–57)— a statement unsupported by empirical biographical "fact" and seemingly symbolic in meaning—is often regarded in its literal sense as a fiction or "beautiful lie," an allegory of the poets pointing to abstract ideological-spiritual "mystical" senses. Usually an annotation is presented of only the assumed abstract anagogical sense of this supposed "beautiful lie," namely, that the poet in his lifetime traveled from the physical world, signified by the supposed fictional term Egypt, to the heavenly Church Triumphant often said to be represented by hosts manifest in the material stellar sphere, signified by the supposed fictional term Jerusalem.

Yet this declaration by Dante's lady (*Par.* XXV, 52–57) is in fact the

FIG. 18. The ambulatory of the sixth-century Constantinian Basilica of San Stefano, Rome. The basilica has been found to be parallel in design to that of Constantine's Holy Sepulchre.

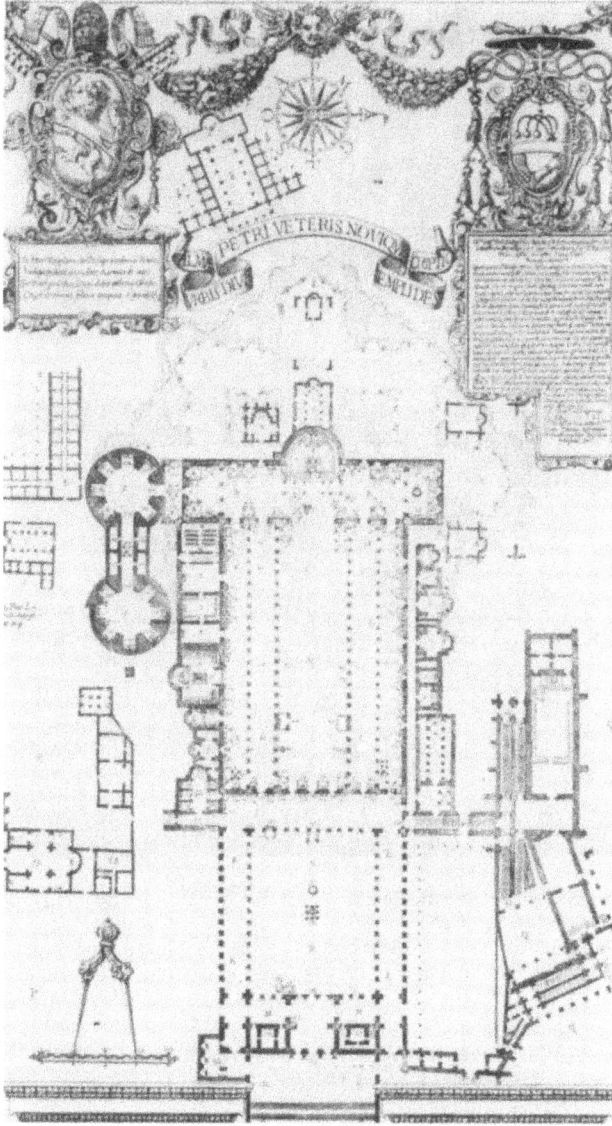

FIG. 19. The Constantinian basilica of Old St. Peter's from a sixteenth-century ground plan by Alpharanus. The basilica in Dante's time included the two circular martyria on the south, columns near the main altar supposedly from Solomon's Temple, and a sixteenth-century wheel-rose in the eastern facade.

clearest and most direct accommodation in all of the *Commedia* of the Exodus theological allegory, disclosed in the passage on Psalm 114 (113 in the Vulgate), of Letter X to Can Grande della Scala, a letter now commonly regarded as written by Dante or reflecting his views. The statement is also one of the clearest and most direct extensions in the poem of the twofold

Fig. 20. The Exodus route across the Red Sea to Mt. Sinai is marked, near the end of the dark Red Sea spur in the upper right, in this twelfth-century "Psalter" mappamundi. Eden appears as a circle containing the heads of Adam and Eve in the East (top); Jerusalem is drawn as a circle at the center. Rome is identified at the lower left of center.

earthly and heavenly typology introduced in final Chapters XL through XLII in Dante's *Vita Nuova*. Are readers, then, in effect being asked to suspend disbelief, to accommodate an "adjustment" in the figural pattern of Dante's life, and to accept that the poet in his "historical" lifetime made *in figura* the earthly Exodus pilgrimage of a Palmer?

That is exactly the point. Displaying a medieval typological consciousness foreign to modern attitudes, Dante orders the details of his past life and of his poetic cosmos to conform with biblical figural patterns, just as he so orders the depiction of his earthly life in the *Vita Nuova* using holy numerological relations and biblical allusions, and just as medieval persons so ordered the structure of the geographic world and of medieval cathedrals by discovering or constructing chains of iconographic "stations" in holy figural arrangements. Through medieval figural back-references of a kind analyzed by Erich Auerbach in discussing souls beyond life in *Dante: Poet*

FIG. 21. The distant summit chapel of Moses, Mt. Sinai, as it actually appeared to medieval pilgrims during their descent of nearby Gebel St. Catherine. Pilgrims faced this view of Mt. Sinai for three to four hours in making their regular pilgrimage "round."

of the Secular World, and by A. C. Charity in discussing the poet in *Events and their Afterlife,* Dante in the literal sense of the *Commedia* discloses that he has made *in figura,* possibly through liturgical-pilgrimage rituals in Rome churches or other Italian churches or perhaps even at "stations" in the Franciscan La Verna region of Tuscany, an earthly figured Egypt-to-Jerusalem Exodus journey that is fulfilled in his pilgrimage beyond life. He thus follows well-established medieval figural traditions in insuring that matter manifests the truths of spirit; and in inventing a work that both embraces and transcends the personal, he graphically illustrates those essential typological biblical patterns to which, he believes, his own life and by inference that of the reader and all persons should conform. And he so joins the great host of actual and legendary medieval "pilgrims" whose journeys to Jerusalem or the Holy Land—journeys made in fact, *in figura,* or recounted in medieval fictional works and oral tradition—gave expression to a spiritual pattern in life aspired to by great numbers of medieval people.

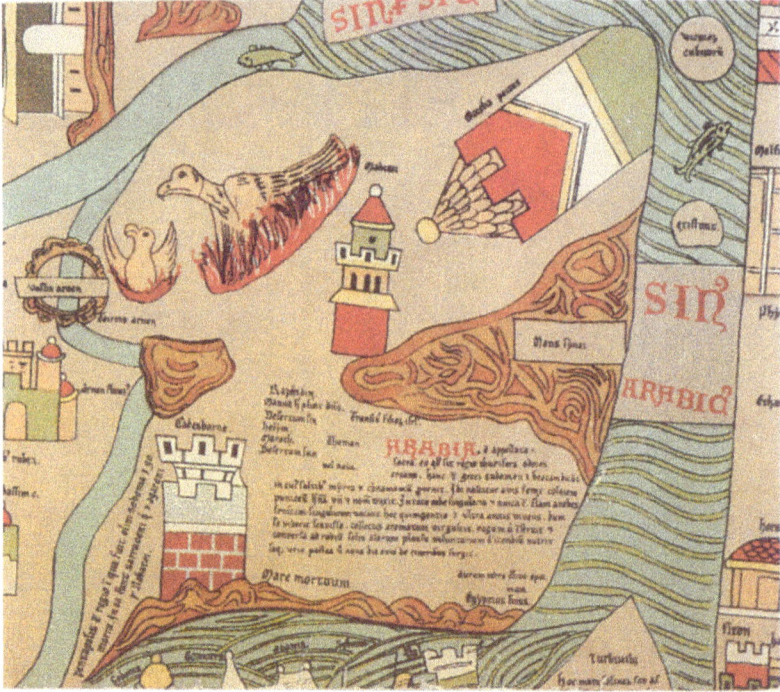

FIG. 22. Detail from the Ebstorf mappamundi (ca. 1235) illustrating the place of the Israelites' Red Sea crossing, Mt. Sinai, and the medieval summit chapel of Moses on the mountain.

Among these "pilgrims" in fact and in medieval legend were St. Francis, St. Jerome, St. Silvia, Paulus Orosius, St. George, King Arthur, Charlemagne, St. Helena, Constantine, and through the centuries the actual Palmers from Italy and other parts of Europe. Included too were those persons who can be associated with Dante, both as figured pilgrims to a "station" of Jerusalem and as "makers" of great medieval figural constructs that pointed the way to the Holy City: Master Builders Jean d'Obais of Rheims and Robert de Luzarches of Amiens. Of course, the ultimate typological model for all actual, figural, and legendary peregrinations of conversion was the original Exodus journey of Moses and the Israelites as recorded in the Bible and as scored by God in the holy sites of the Sinai.

Like the dead souls in the *Commedia* whose existence in the other world can be seen as an extension in an altered state of previous mortal life, Dante's foreshadowed earthly life—gradually remembered and revealed as an acted out past sequence of ever more holy biblical-pilgrimage events serving as types—is continued and intensified through the poet's repeated acting out in the remembered "present" of the same sequence of events now uplifted to a transcendent, other-worldly plane and serving as antitypes. Dante obviously differs from the dead souls in that he is alive. But in an audacious poetic maneuver, the poet in his role as pilgrim imposes

FIG. 23. The stone Gate of Confession, and some of the approximately 3,400 stone steps, on the medieval pilgrimage pathway up Mt. Sinai to the summit chapel of Moses.

upon this foreshadowed world and upon the imagined details of the realms beyond—realms that he nonetheless obviously believes are actually there—the deep-rooted medieval experience of "true" existence as a continuing imitation in body and soul, in appropriate locales, of the same crucial, biblical episodes in universal Hebraic-Christian history. Through recurrent participation in the cyclical calendar of church services centered on Easter, through recurrent actual or figured pilgrimage to holy sites, through meditation on the cycle of holy occurrences in divine revelation, the same scriptural events were imitated again and again; and such actions, when constantly performed in ever more virtuous fashion under the illumination of grace, were thought to transport a few extraordinary mortals to the spiritual

Photograph by P. DEAN

FIG. 24. In accord with the traditional Exodus route recorded in pilgrim texts from the fourth century and first defined in terms of "stations" in the twelfth century, the line of the Exodus is fully drawn (upper right) on the Hereford mappamundi (ca. 1285). The line moves across the Red Sea to illustrated Mt. Sinai, loops down and around the Mare Mortuum, and then ends to the southeast of the central circle of Jerusalem. Eden, directly above Jerusalem, and Rome are marked in their usual locations. The labyrinth of Crete, a former pagan navel of the world, is clearly visible in the Mare Internum on the sea route between Rome and Egypt. The map is believed to have guided medieval persons making long great circle pilgrimages.

The pilgrim Fetellus, in a twelfth-century *Descriptio* still in use as a pilgrim guide book in the seventeenth century, identified forty-two "stations" of the Exodus along a pathway corresponding to that on the Hereford map. Anonymous pilgrim VI in the twelfth century made the same identifications.

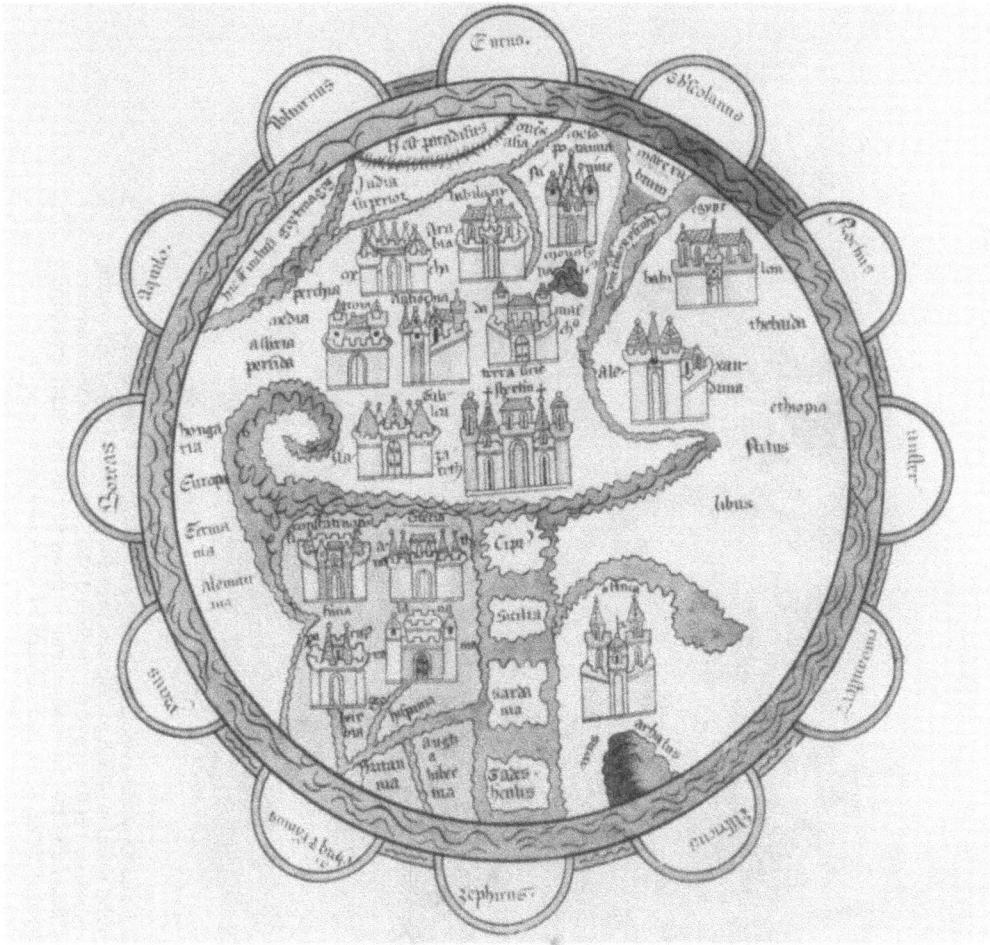

FIG. 25. Mappamundi (ca. 1380) from the *Grandes Chroniques de St. Denis* showing "Babylon" in Egypt, the Red Sea, Mt. Sinai (upper right to left), Jerusalem (center), Rome (lower left-center), and Paris (lower left).

level of the angels in eternity. Each repeated fulfillment of biblical history in the life of an individual, moreover, was in itself necessarily a true, historical event. And from the literal sense of Dante's past foreshadowing pilgrimage in life, as well as from the literal sense of the poet's "present" journey beyond life affording fulfillment on a higher spiritual plane—both the past types and the "present" anti-types being considered in their sequential unfolding as historically "true"—the same senses of the Exodus, outlined in Letter X, arise: the allegorical sense (serving as the figural in theological allegory) pointing to the historical Redemption through Christ; the moral sense signifying abstractly the conversion of the soul from sin to grace; and the anagogical sense, signifying abstractly the movement of the soul from the corruption of this world to the eternal glory of heaven.

FIG. 26. On this Osma Beatus T-and-O world iconographic map (ca. 1203), the heads of the twelve Apostles, each in the nation of the world in which the Apostle preached, surround the central region of the Holy Land and Jerusalem situated at the top of the darkened Mare Internum or Mediterranean Sea. The curved River Jordan flows into the Mare Mortuum or Dead Sea in the Sinai area (upper right). The map illustrated Beatus of Valcavado's commentary on the Apocalypse.

II. THE TEMPLE, WHEELS AND ROSE OF HEAVEN: TRANSFIGURATION AND THE COSMIC BOOK

It is the radiant eyes of Beatrice that lead Dante on the journey of his life to the Cosmic Book unified in God. In Eden the eyes dazzlingly shimmer "like the sun in a mirror" (*Purg.* XXXI, 121: "Come in lo specchio il sol") with the twofold form of a holy beast, the Griffon, signifying Christ. Among the fixed stars these eyes, beaming vast distances, give to Dante's own vision a startling and transcendent clarity:

> così de li occhi miei ogne quisquilia
> fugò Beatrice col raggio d'i suoi,
> che rifulgea da più di mille milia
>
> (*Par.* XXVI, 76–78)

> so Beatrice dissipated every mote
> from my eyes with the ray of her own
> that shone for more than a thousand miles.

In a passage of extraordinary poetic power, they flash in the Primum Mobile "as a taper's flame in glass" (*Par.* XXVIII, 4: "come in lo specchio fiamma di doppiero") with the reversed image of the entire physical universe. And the eyes of Beatrice last gaze down upon Dante, before turning to the eternal fountain of light, from the distant celestial rose. So clear is Dante's vision of Beatrice in this immaterial realm that the poet writes, "her image descended to me not mingled with any medium" (*Par.* XXXI, 77–78: "süa effige/non discendëa a me per mezzo mista").

The radiance in Beatrice's eyes, like the lesser glow in other substances, is of a special kind. When Dante early in the *Paradiso* asks his lady about the light passing through the partially translucent and yet spotted substance of the moon, Beatrice replies that the moon does not reflect light as do medieval looking glasses composed of "glass which hides lead behind itself" (*Par.* II, 89–90: "vetro/lo qual di retro a sé piombo nasconde"). Rather, she offers a metaphysical explanation. "Divers virtues make divers alloy" (*Par.* II, 139: "Virtù diversa fa diversa lega"), Beatrice explains,

> Per la natura lieta onde deriva,
> la virtù mista per lo corpo luce
> come letizia per pupilla viva.
> Da essa vien ciò che da luce a luce
> par differente, non da denso e raro
>
> (*Par.* II, 142–146)

61

Because of the glad nature from which
   it flows, the mingled virtue shines
   through the body as gladness does through a living pupil.
Thence comes what seems different between light and light
   not from density and rarity

It is the virtue of the object, not its physical constitution, that determines
the level of its spiritual illumination.

Later in the Primum Mobile when telling Dante how the three-fold light
of God instantaneously created the angels just as light passes instantaneously through glass and virtuous stones, Beatrice on this occasion adds
no comment about the "vetro" or glass being on one side coated with lead
to form on the other a reflective surface. She instead uses the word "vetro"
in its primary sense to denote a virtuous transparent substance which light
illumines and through which it is conveyed:

E come in vetro, in ambra o in cristallo
   raggio risplende sì, che dal venire
   a l'esser tutto non è intervallo;
così 'l triforme effetto del suo sire
   ne l'esser suo raggiò insieme tutto,
   senza distinzïone in essordire.

(Par. XXIX, 25–30)

and as in glass, in amber, or in crystal, a ray
   so glows that there is no interval from its
   coming to its prevading all;
so the threefold effect rayed out all
   at once from its Lord into its being,
   without distinction of beginning.

Though the radiance of Beatrice's eyes like that of glass must be understood in a metaphysical sense, John Leyerle and James L. Miller have persuasively advanced an interrelated philosophic-naturalistic explanation—
one based upon the thirteenth-century optical knowledge of Roger Bacon,
Albertus Magnus, Thomas Aquinas and others—of the peculiar power of
this lady's eyes to be internally illumined and to reflect, transmit, focus,
and "ray" divine light.[46] Dante's lady, they maintain, gazes with optical

---

[46] Leyerle, "The Rose-Wheel Design and Dante's *Paradiso*," 280–307; and Miller, "Three
Mirrors of Dante's *Paradiso*," *University of Toronto Quarterly* 46, number 3 (Spring, 1977):
261–279. A recent and most revealing analysis of mirror images in selected medieval works
appears in V. A. Kolve, *Chaucer and the Imagery of Narrative*, 52–60. Historical background
on knowledge of optics in the twelfth century can be found in A. C. Crombie, *Robert Grosseteste
and the Origins of Experimental Science: 1100–1170* (Oxford, 1953).

It needs to be observed that Dante's analogic and metaphoric references particularly relating
to mirror images in general point to a language that—through ever more tenuous yet brilliantly
chosen intermediary analogies, metaphors, and allusions—captures by "degrees" a limited
and glancing discursive or intuitive apprehension of what are regarded as transcendent objects

powers discovered by Robert Grosseteste (ca. 1168–1253) and largely embodied by medieval glaziers in the layered "specula," optical glasses or
lenses, that conveyed sharp beams of heavenly light through lofty "rota-
rosa" windows down to worshippers in twelfth and thirteenth-century
cathedrals. The round transept windows at Lincoln Cathedral, Leyerle notes,
were actually referred to as the "two eyes of the church" ("Ecclesiae due
sont oculi") in an anonymously written thirteenth-century poem on the
life of St. Hugh, Bishop of Lincoln.[47]

Knowledgeable references to optics appear in a number of late medieval
literary works, the most notable being Jean de Meun's continuation of the
Roman de la Rose (ca. 1280). In Prosa IV of the continued poem, the author
introduces the figure Nature who, in presenting a discourse on optics, explains the many optical effects resulting from light striking or passing
through glass which is transparent, polished, coated on one side, or formed
into different kinds of lenses. The discourse has rightly been interpreted
as suggesting that the poem itself, referred to as a "miroure" by Jean de
Meun, is both a reflecting glass and a lens radiating and deflecting light
upon love and lovers.[48]

---

beyond direct, full human knowledge. Scholastic and Thomistic philosophic attitudes, joined
with medieval mystical theology, clearly govern Dante's linguistic practices. Recently Jacques
Maritain, adopting such philosophic and mystical views toward language in an analysis employing references to mirrors, has called attention in *The Degrees of Knowledge,* trans. under
Gerald B. Phelan from the fourth French edition (New York, 1959) to how, from the Thomistic
outlook, transcendent objects or "transobjective subjects" which "do not fall at first within
our grasp . . . are known by the intermediary of the primordially apprehended analogate.
They are known in the latter as in a mirror," Maritain continues, "in virtue of the likeness it
has with them. This is specular knowledge or knowledge by analogy. . . . Strictly speaking,
the transobjective subjects in which they are realized are not *subject* to our intelligible grasps,
do not *give themselves up* to us as objects. It is not their essence or their first intelligible
constitutive which is objectivized for us by means of our presentative forms and concepts.
They are known, however, intrinsically and properly designed, constituted as objects of in-
tellection, but as it were at a distance and not in themselves. The ray of the intellect that
attains them has been refracted or reflected, and they always remain above the knowledge
we have of them, superior to the grasps that reach up to them, separated from our mind in
the very act which unites it to them" (pp. 210–211).

See Étienne Gilson, *Dante the Philosopher,* trans. David Moore (London, 1948) on Dante's
individualized integration of traditional elements in classical philosophy, medieval rational
theology, and medieval mystical theology.

[47] The poem written about 1225–1235 contains the lines:

Praebentes geminae jubar orbiculare fenestrae,
Ecclesiae due sunt oculi: recteque videtur
Major in his esse praesul, minor esse decanus.

The twin windows exhibiting a circular splendour
are the two eyes of the church;
and the larger of them is rightly seen to
be the bishop and the smaller, the dean.

The poem was printed in the last century under the title *The Metrical Life of St. Hugh, Bishop
of Lincoln,* ed. J. F. Demcock (London, 1860), 35–36; and the lines cited above are quoted and
translated by Leyerle in "The Rose Wheel," 293.

[48] See Patricia J. Eberle, "The Lovers' Looking Glass: Nature's Discourse on Optics and the
Optical Design of the Romance of the Rose," *University of Toronto Quarterly* 46, number 3

Dante's use of the words "speglio," "specchio," and "speculum," given
poetic contexts and medieval meanings, also appears usually to connote
both a reflective "looking glass" and a transparent "optical glass" or lens.
When Beatrice's eyes in the Primum Mobile are compared to a "specchio"
(*Par.* XXVIII, 4), for example, Dante seems to be signifying that they simultaneously retain, mirror, and "beam" light in accord with their metaphysical virtue but also in a way consonant with the optical knowledge of
the period. Yet the radiance of Beatrice's eyes would doubtless have been
widely suggestive to early readers, calling to consciousness an unearthly
medieval metal mirror that is forever untarnished, or a crystal prism through
which light rays, or a stained glass window panel transformed by internal
or external darkness from a lens into a bright, reflective surface. And always
Beatrice's eyes would be observed to glimmer with the light of God's love
and grace.

Dante's more general "rota" and light icons, embracing and synthesizing
the physical universe mirrored in Beatrice's eyes and the figured "wheels"
of the celestial city and of Godhead, surely have medieval architectural
sources. Throughout Italy, Europe and the Near East, the perfect circles of
the earthly "rota-rosa" windows, as numerous commentators have confirmed, manifested the entire cosmos, the concentric rings with a divine
image at their center often containing *figurae* variously showing the earthly
paradise, moon, planets, sun, stars, zodiac, and immaterial heavens. The
"rosa" form of the windows by tradition signified both the Virgin Mary
and heavenly love; and translucent colored icons of the Virgin, frequently
appearing in the center or summit panels of the windows, glowed in the
heavenly light that also illumined other panels traditionally depicting Old
and New Testament personages. The "rota" with its tracery of spokes and
petals, conceived of as a complex geometrical-theological model of divine
cosmic order, signified too the dynamic nature of an active, creative Godhead and universe. Uplifted high in the cathedral facade and transepts,
the "rota-rosa" windows as types of the cosmos both fulfilled and subsumed
the circular icons of just the physical earth represented in T-and-O altar
icons and in the round "mazes" inlaid in stone in the nave floor.

Just as Dante gave form to the iconography of the Book of the World in
the *Commedia* by using the popular literature of "spiritual geography" and
pilgrimage, he gave form to the transcendent Book of the Cosmos in his
poem employing the popular art of cathedral architecture.

Inspired as was Abbot Suger, builder of the "first" Gothic cathedral St.
Denis, by celestial cosmographers including St. Paul and Pseudo-Dionysius,
Dante in the immaterial Primum Mobile poetically constructs a "wondrous
and angelic temple" (*Par.* XXVIII, 53: "miro e angelico templo") according
to the divine order manifest in musical harmony and in the metrics of

---

(Spring, 1977): 241–262. Optical references, as Eberle notes, are used to establish points-of-
view in the *Roman de la Rose* and in a medieval work such as the satirical *Speculum stultorum*
(ca. 1190), the "Fools' Glass," also known as *The Book of Burnellus the Ass.*

number, "as a song with its measure" (*Par.* XXVIII, 9: "come nota con suo metro"). Author Dante, taking his inspiration from the "perfect" architectural forms of the classical and Byzantine Orient, creates a transcendent temple having "only love and light for boundary" (*Par.* XXVIII, 54: "solo amore e luce ha per confine") of a kind of which Suger could only dream.

Dante's vision of the cosmic temple comes just after the poet, in the lower sphere of the fixed stars, has viewed pilgrimage routes in the physical world and has been told by his lady of the Egypt-to-Jerusalem foreshadowing segment of his long pilgrimage. Now having ascended to the Primum Mobile, Dante with a mind "imparadised" by his lady (*Par.* XXVIII, 3), experiences a wider vision of the physical book of the universe that has its being in God. It is at this juncture that the poet sees what is called the "volume" (*Par.* XXVIII, 14) of the material cosmos reflected, reversed, and glowing like a flame from his lady's eyes.

In a passage of extraordinary economy and striking poetic power, Dante describes how he turns his gaze from the eyes of Beatrice to a "temple" that gives form to the physical universe:

> come in lo specchio fiamma di doppiero
> vede colui che se n'alluma retro,
> prima che l'abbia in vista o in pensiero,
> e sé rivolge per veder se 'l vetro
> li dice il vero, e vede ch'el s'accorda
> con esso come nota con suo metro;
> così la mia memoria si ricorda
> ch'io feci riguardando ne' belli occhi,
> onde a pigliarmi fece Amor la corda.
> E com' io mi rivolsi e furon tocchi
> li miei da ciò che pare in quel volume,
> quandunque nel suo giro ben s'adocchi,
> un punto vidi che raggiava lume
> acuto sì, che 'l viso ch'elli effoca,
> chiuder conviensi per lo forte acume;

(*Par.* XXVIII, 4–18)

> as one who sees in a mirror a taper's flame
> lighted behind him before he has it
> in sight or in thought
> and turns around to see whether the glass
> tells the truth, and sees that it accords
> with it as song with its measure,
> so my memory recalls that I did,
> gazing into the beautiful eyes in which
> Love made the noose to capture me;
> and when I turned, and my own were met
> by what appears in that volume whenever
> one gazes intently on its circling;

> a point I saw that rayed forth light so keen
> that the vision on which it blazes needs
> must close because of its strong power;

Dante now observes one-by-one, in an unfolding vision, nine angelic circles of fire that comprise the temple whirling around the penetrating point of brightness; the inmost and brightest circle wheeling so rapidly that it surpasses in speed the motion of the outermost and fastest moving sphere of the physical universe; the other angelic circles turning at ever slower speeds in proportion to their increasing distance from the central light. Dante sees that in the physical universe the reverse is true; the innermost corporeal spheres move at ever slower speeds in accord with their nearness to the earth.

The poet understands at once that the immaterial angelic temple is the "model" or "essemplo," the physical universe its "copy" or "essemplare" (*Par.* XXVIII, 55–56); but he expresses puzzlement over why the movements of these circular immaterial and material divine constructs differ. In answer to a question by Dante, Beatrice declares that in the physical universe, the outermost spheres have greater speed because possessed of greater virtue in accord with their greater size; while in the angelic temple, the innermost spheres closest to the central light have the most virtue and spiritual brightness and so move with the greatest rapidity. But even in this inversion of speeds and virtues, Beatrice perceives a marvelous correspondence in design.

> tu vederai mirabil consequenza
> di maggio a più e di minore a meno,
> in ciascun cielo, a süa intelligenza.
>
> (Par. XXVIII, 76–78)

> You will see a marvelous agreement of greater
> to more and of smaller to less, in each
> heaven with respect to its Intelligence.

And identifying the intense point of light with Godhead, she announces that "On that point the heavens and all nature are dependent" (*Par.* XXVIII, 41–42: "Da quel punto/ depende il cielo e tutta la natura").

Dante's vision of the angelic temple directs the reader's awareness backward but also forward to a figurally related sequence of light icons, disclosed within or through the movements of Beatrice's circular eyes, that are manifest as ever more distinguishable and more dazzlingly illumined concentric circles and points of brightness. The foreshadowed and fulfilled light icons lead Dante spiritually upward from the reflected image of the griffin, blazing in his lady's round eyes as the sun in a looking glass, and seen in the round "nido" or "nest" (*Purg.* XXVIII, 78) of Eden figuring Jerusalem; to the penultimate vision of Godhead that is first observed as a single flame and then as three rotating circles of light. After leaving the Earthly Paradise, Dante at the beginning of *Paradiso* had followed Beatrice's gaze aloft, "like a pilgrim whose will is to return" (*Par.* I, 51: "pur come pelegrin che tornar vuole"), to the luminescence of the round sun. In the sphere of this orb with his power of sight increased through the "splendor" of his lady's eyes (*Par.* X, 62), he had witnessed twin sparkling circles of dancers including respectively St. Francis and St. Benedict, circles that wheeled about himself and his lady "like stars neighbouring the fixed poles" (*Par.* X, 78: "come stelle vicine a' fermi poli"). And in this realm he had seen again, now at closer range, the blazing sun. "Give thanks, give thanks," Beatrice had asserted, "to the sun of the Angels, who of his grace that to this sun of sense exalted you" (*Par.* X, 52–54: "Ringrazia,/ ringrazia il Sol de li angeli, ch'a questo/ sensibil t'ha levato per sua grazia"). Among the stars the poet had been briefly blinded when the Apostle St. John approached nearer still like "the sun eclipsed a little" (*Par.* XXV, 119: "eclissar lo sole un poco"). The icons of the physical sun that signify divine light, each icon prefiguring the next, are largely fulfilled in the Primum Mobile in the concentrated point of spiritual light mirrored in Beatrice's eyes, a light that foreshadows the final, refulgent, circular icon of Beatific Vision.

The progressively developed figurism of the *Commedia* also explicitly reveals the circular iconographic "copies," in both the physical Book of the Cosmos and the lesser earthly Book of the World, of the round, immaterial "model" temple of the angels. The nested spheres of the universe of sense or "mondo sensibile" (*Par.* XXVIII, 49) are, the typology of the poem implies, a grand, cosmic physical temple formed after the angelic original; yet the temples of the angels and of the material spheres are in turn prefigured in the circular "nest" of Eden, at the center of the southern hemisphere, that contains types of the Old and New "circular" Temples in what was considered the circular city of Jerusalem. Dante thus created the angelic temple, not according to the Latin cruciform plan, but following the circular classical-Byzantine design used both in the medieval Old Temple and in the Anastasis of the New Temple of the Holy Sepulchre and in their figural replication in Italy and Europe. And at the center of the angelic temple, Dante placed the point of light, surrounded by moving circles of sparks and signifying Godhead, that through typology refers forward to the central light and nested circles of the Beatific Vision just as it refers back to the tomb of Christ at the center of the nested-circle design of the Holy Sepulchre's Anastasis. The angelic temple's point of light can even be seen to refer back farther still to the monstrous, antithetical type of all that is unholy: to Satan entombed at the earth's center at the core of the infernal city Dis that is the figural opposite of the heavenly city of the rose.

It has been shown that Dante meets Beatrice, a type of Christ, in the figured setting of the Old Temple on sacred Mt. Sion. When the poet in Eden faces east toward the point of the rising sun, he observes the divine pageant accompanying Beatrice glide into view at the moment dazzling light flashes and heavenly voices sing "*Osanna*" (*Purg.* XXIX, 51). This is the chant cried out by the multitude—as recorded in the Gospels of Matthew, Mark, and John—when Christ descended the Mt. of Olives, climbed

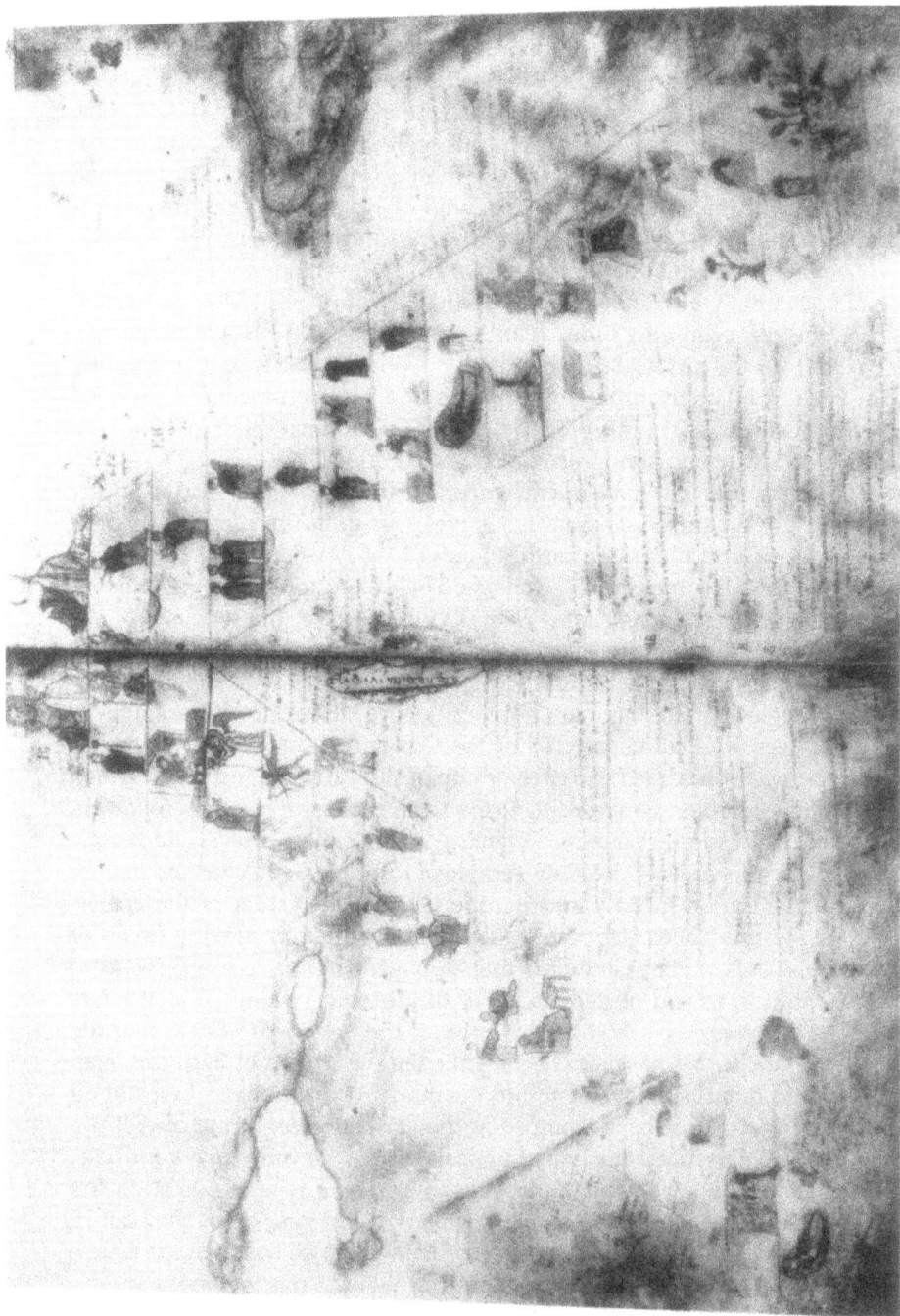

the western hill of Mt. Sion, and entered into the Old Temple enclosure of Jerusalem. It is also the chant sung by the nine angelic orders, in the fulfilled round angelic temple of the Primum Mobile, as they move in perfect circles about the central light of Godhead (*Par.* XXVIII, 94). In terrestrial Eden Dante has been shown to proceed in procession with Beatrice from the figured site of the Old Temple to a place where Eden's tree of life is crossed by a spar of the chariot of the Church, a place of the Cross signifying the New Temple of the Holy Sepulchre that enclosed both the traditional Golgotha, with the alleged burial site of Adam's skull beneath, and the traditional tomb of Christ.[49] Voices in Eden murmur the name "Adamo" (*Purg.* XXXII, 37) just before the tree is crossed by the chariot's spar, thus emphasizing the Redemptive nature of the Cross of Jerusalem in overcoming the sin of this First Parent. The New Temple of the Holy Sepulchre in fact also sheltered the cleft rock through which Christ's blood

---

[49] In *Itinerarium Burdigalense*, ed. P. Geyer and O. Cuntz in *Itineraria et Alia Geographica: Corpus Christianorum, Series Latina*, vol. 175 (Città del Vaticano, 1965), 15–16, the pilgrim from Burdigala, now Bordeaux, outlines in the fourth century the Jerusalem city route from the Old Temple to the New on a line parallel to modern King David Street. And in *Itinerarium Egeriae*, ed. E. Franceschini and R. Weber in *Itineraria et Alia Geographica*, vol. 175 as cited above, pp. 77–78, Egeria (St. Silvia) also in the fourth century describes a Palm Sunday procession moving down the Mount of Olives, through the Golden Gate in the Eastern wall of Jerusalem, and then on from the Old Temple to the new. Stephen Graham in *With the Russian Pilgrims to Jerusalem* (London, 1916), 241–243, records in this century Palm Sunday liturgical practices in Jerusalem that still follow the patterns outlined by Egeria. Such Palm Sunday practices remain in use in the Holy City today.

Illustrations of eleventh- and twelfth-century circular iconographic maps of Jerusalem of a kind still popular in Dante's time—maps showing the city as a cross within a circle, the Old Temple usually as a circle, and the New Temple as a circle surmounted by a cross—are reproduced in Sabino de Sondoli's *Itinera Hierosolymitana Crucesignatorum*, vol. 2, pp. 391, 413, and 422.

FIG. 27. Detailed eleventh-century geographic icon of Mt. Sinai, shown in its traditional mappamundi location between the Mare Mortuum (left of center) and the Red Sea (dark projection on the right), with personages on the mountain's steps to God serving as exempla of specific virtues and vices. The icon appears as the table of contents for a manuscript, in the monastery at Patmos, of Sinai Bishop John Climacus's *Scala Paradisi*, the Greek work translated into Latin in the Franciscan Mount La Verna region of Italy in the late thirteenth century. Beneath God on the top-right step, a monk receives the crown or wreath of Charity from an angel. On other steps to the right, Avarice is represented by a seated personage (eighth from top), and Gluttony by a personage at a table (ninth from top). On steps to the left, Pride is seen as a monk in a cave being assailed by a devil (fourth from top), Lust as a personage attacked by another devil (eighth from top), and Penitence as a monk in the gate of a cell (third from bottom).

The pilgrimage pathway up the mountain of Exodus, a figural type for Dante's Mt. Purgatory, was described through the centuries in numerous western pilgrim tracts beginning with that of St. Silvia (St. Etheria) in the fourth century. At the monastery of St. Catherine, Mt. Sinai, medieval pilgrims who spoke different languages, but who were joined together by the common experience of ascending the holy mountain's stone stairs, could view many early icons depicting the ladder to God.

was said by pilgrims to have flowed down from the Cross, supposedly made from the wood of the tree of life, upon the skull of Adam below.[50] Both the Old and New round Temples of Jerusalem were restored in the Middle Ages to contain nested rings of stations about which pilgrims and others circled, in imperfect but solemn imitation of divine movements like those of the angels, to the holiest points at the center; respectively, the rock of the altar of Solomon and the tomb of Christ both of which were venerated as sources of spiritual light.

When Dante initially writes of seeing the angelic temple mirrored in Beatrice's eyes, he appears to refer to the Knights Templar who, until the destruction of their order in 1310, took oaths to protect the Holy Sepulchre and other holy shrines and who, in medieval myth, were said to have been the builders of Latin cruciform glass temples such as Chartres.[51] Earlier on Mt. Purgatory's terrace of the avaricious, Dante had heard Hugh Capet denounce French King Philip the Fair, the leader of the successful movement to crush the Templars and to take possession of their holdings, as the "novo Pilato" or "new Pilate" who "bears his greedy sails into the temple" (*Purg.* XX, 93: "portar nel Tempio le cupide vele"). Then in the Primum Mobile of *Paradiso* Dante, in looking from the ideal immaterial angelic temple back to Beatrice, confirms that he has accurately seen its reversed and reflected image in her "beautiful eyes in which love had made the noose to capture me" (XXVIII, 11–12: "belli occhi/ onde a pigliarmi fece Amor la corda").

The "corda" here appears to be the rope of honor worn by the Templars rather than the Franciscan "capestro," or cord of humility, that serves as a girdle for the Franciscan Guido da Montefeltro in the *Inferno* (XXVII, 92).[52] Dante is captured by the divine love that bound the knights to their vows as guardians of the Jerusalem temple. The power of Beatrice's eyes over the poet is accordingly comparable to the power of the "corda" or "noose" that, for the Templars, symbolized their military duty to overcome or to capture the infidel, or to die rather than suffer defeat.

---

[50] Allusions to the skull of Adam buried beneath Golgotha appear, for example, in two twelfth-century pilgrim texts: *The Pilgrimage of the Russian Abbot Daniel in the Holy Land*, trans. Aubrey Stewart, notes C. W. Wilson (London, 1895), 15; and Anonymous Pilgrim VI in *Anonymous Pilgrims, I–VIII*, trans. Aubrey Steward (London, 1894), 22. For recent studies comparing episodes and places in Dante's Eden to those in Jerusalem as it was known in the poet's time, see note 9.

A pagan altar dedicated to Adam, an altar pre-dating Roman shrines to Venus and later Christian shrines, was unearthed in the Hill of Calvary within the Holy Sepulchre in the 1970s as the result of excavations sponsored by the Greek Orthodox Patriarch, Jerusalem. See Christos Kalsimbinis, *The Uncovering of the Eastern Side of the Hill of Calvary and its Base* (Jerusalem, 1977), 197–208.

[51] See Painton Cowen, *Rose Windows*, 100.

[52] St. Francis's disciple Illuminato, who accompanied the saint to the Holy Land, is said along with Augustine to have worn the "capestro" in *Par.* XII, 132. The early follower of St. Francis, Silvestro, is also identified as wearing a "capestro" in *Par.* XI, 87. See the recent discussion of the "corda" and the "capestro" in Helmut Hatzfeld, "Modern Literary Scholarship as Reflected in Dante Criticism," 206–207; and William Anderson, *Dante the Maker*, 362–363.

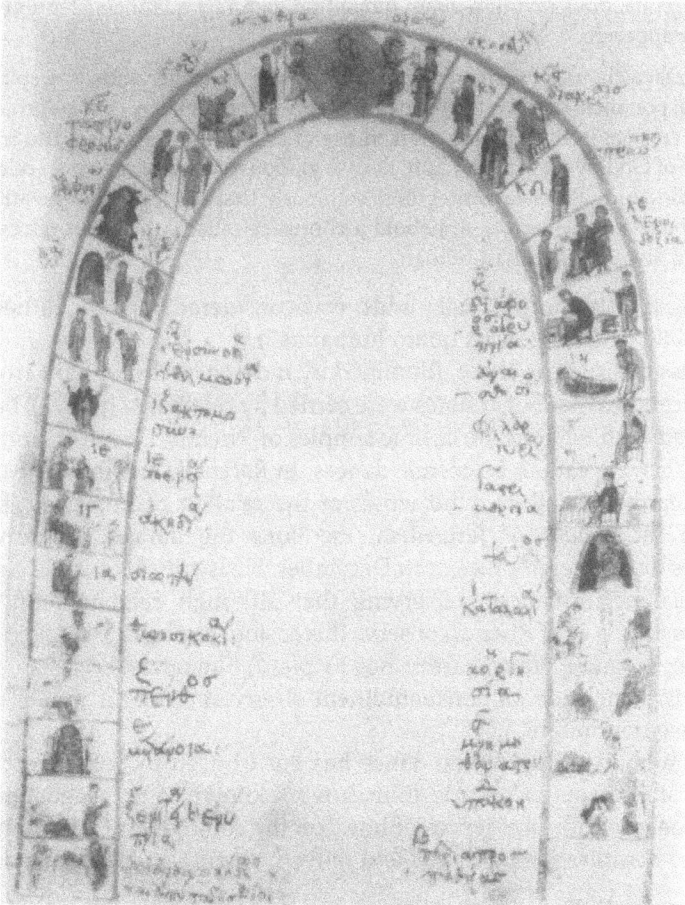

FIG. 28. In a late twelfth or early thirteenth-century Vatican library manuscript of the *Scala Paradisi*, the steps and personages appear in the table of contents arranged in the same order as in the Patmos manuscript. The ladder is bent apparently to provide room for captions.

Circular processions and actual dances in earthly "temple" cathedrals came to be associated with transcendent celestial movements of a kind Dante describes in the angelic temple. Under the influence of the "angelic" theology of pseudo-Dionysius, Abbot Suger writes in *De Consecratione* (ca. 1146), for example, of a seemingly celestial "chorus" proceeding round and round the upper choir of the St. Denis "temple," the area between the nave and the main altar, during the Great Consecration on 11 June 1144. Suger enthusiastically declaims upon

tot tantorum choream pontificum vestibus albis decoram, mitris pontificalibus et circinatis aurifrisiis pretiosis admodum comatam, pastorales virgas manibus tenere, circumcirca dolium ambire, nomen Domini exorcizando invocare; tan gloriosos et admirabiles viros aeterni sponsi nuptias tam pie celebrare, ut potius chorus coelestis

quam terrenus, opus divinum quam humanum, tam regi quam assistenti nobilitati
videretur apparere.[53]

how so great a chorus of such great pontiffs, decorous in white vestments, splendidly
arrayed in pontifical miters and precious orphreys embellished by circular ornaments,
held the crosiers in their hands, walked round and round the vessel and invoked
the name of God by way of exorcism; how so glorious and admirable men celebrated
the wedding of the Eternal Bridegroom so piously that the King and the attending
nobility believed themselves to behold a chorus celestial rather than terrestrial, a
ceremony divine rather than human.

The song of this chorus, Suger adds, was considered "angelic rather than
human" ("potius angelicus quam humanus").[54]

Processions such as these, illumined by moving circles of light from the
flaming candles that Suger notes were carried by celebrants (p. 117), became
associated with what in the cosmic temples of Rheims, Chartres, and other
cathedrals were said to be cosmic dances. In *Rationale divinorum officiorum*
(1164) Joannes Belethus, who writes of the relation of liturgy to the pilgrimage "stationes" of Jerusalem, mentions the dances performed in
churches during ceremonies each December. He is critical of these custom-
ary dance performances, observing that although celebrants in "great
churches, that is as of Rheims, observe this custom of playing, it nevertheless
seems to be more praiseworthy not to play" ("magnae Ecclesiae, ut est
Remensis, hanc-ludendi consuetudinem observent, videtur tamen lauda-
bilius esse non ludere").[55]

The tradition of the divine dance has been traced by John Freccero to
the Gnostic Gospel of pseudo-John, a work known to St. Augustine.[56] In
this gospel pseudo-John writes of how, on the command of Christ, he and
the other disciples joined hands and moved, singing and dancing, around

---

[53] *Abbot Suger on the Abbey Church of St.-Denis and its Art Treasures*, trans. and notes Erwin
Panofsky, 2nd ed., ed. Gerda Panofsky-Soergel (Princeton, 1979), 114–115. See also the
account of the thirteenth-century reconstruction of the building in Caroline A. Bruzelius, *The
Thirteenth-Century Church at St. Denis* (New Haven and London, 1986).

[54] *Abbot Suger*, 121.

[55] See Chapter CXX of that work in *Patrologiae Cursus Completus*, vol. 202, 2nd series, ed.
J. P. Migne (Paris, 1885), 125. Belethus in chapter VI, pp. 18–19 discusses the liturgy and the
pilgrimage stations in Jerusalem. See also the historical and critical study of cosmic and sacred
dances in James Lester Miller, "Vision of the Cosmic Dance in Western Literature from Plato
to Jean de Meun," University of Toronto Doctoral Dissertation, 1979. Erwin Mehal in "Der
Ausweg aus dem Labyrinth," *Festgabe für Leopold Schmidt* (Wien, 1972) cites a relatively late
example of sacred labyrinth dances, performed in 1412, involving members of the convent
at Auxerre in the cathedral of that city. On the basis of the text of the early *Ordinatio de pila
facienda*, Mehal explains how chanting performers first moved around the cathedral labyrinth
floor and then joined in an ensemble dance (pp. 402ff.).

[56] "The Dance of the Stars: *Paradiso X,*" *Dante: The Poetics of Conversion*, 229–231. In examining the history of holy classical, Hebraic, and Christian "earth dances in consonance
with heaven," John C. Meagher in "The Dance in the Masques of Jonson," *Journal of the
Warburg and Courtault Institute* 25 (1962): 258–270, analyzes sacred dance passages in the
Gnostic *Acts of John* and in texts by Caelius Rhodiginus, Menestrier, Lucian, Plotinus, St. Basil,
and other writers.

FIG. 29. St. Francis receives the Stigmata on Mt. La Verna, the Italian type of Holy Land mountains Sinai and Sion, in this thirteenth-century fresco by Giotto, San Francesco, Assisi. On Mt. La Verna the Franciscans established a pilgrimage path with stone stairs and "stations" that replicated such sacred pilgrimage-mountain paths guarded by the order in the Holy Land. In *Paradiso* XI, Dante writes of the "crudo sasso" of La Verna on which St. Francis was marked with "l'ultimo sigillo."

the Savior who stood at the center. The twelve disciples and their dance were then compared in Judaeo-Hellenic tradition to the twelve moving signs of the zodiac. In Dante's period the tradition of celestial song and dance had become a motif in architectural iconography as well as in popular and religious ritual. In the dynamic wheel-rose window designs signifying circular motion, the twelve apostles were often depicted on the inner petals of the rose; the corresponding signs of the zodiac on the outer petals; and Christ at the hub or center. Ceremonies on the labyrinth floors or altars below were then conducted in figural imitation of the divine order and movement represented by the cosmic wheels above.

FIG. 30. On the central entrance tympanum of St. Denis, hovering angels bear Passion relics supposedly presented to the church by Charlemagne following his legendary pilgrimage with twelve nobles to Jerusalem. A dominating Christ Incarnate, with arms outspread on the cross, appears beneath the angels.

FIG. 31. In the luminous glass-and-stone "temple" of St. Denis harboring the supposed tomb of the theologian of light Pseudo-Dionysius, translucent screens of glass radiate light through the reconstructed south transept wheel-rose, showing New Testament personages, and through the reconstructed windows of the south clerestory. Abbot Suger, supervising the construction in the twelfth century of this "first" Gothic cathedral, erected twelve columns which he described in his *De Administratione* as "representing the number of the twelve Apostles." Suger, who stated in his book that he conversed with pilgrims from Jerusalem, wrote also of "columns in the side-aisles signifying the number of the Prophets." Suger's "temple," like Dante's *Paradiso*, was created under the strong influence of Pseudo-Dionysius' *De Caelesti Hierarchia* and of Byzantine-Romanesque "temple" figurism.

Although Suger was extremely conscious of the figural significance of holy liturgical movement, he described the St. Denis consecration procession as taking place in a choir that was constructed as a rectangle. Circular processions of seemingly celestial participants, executed to song amid the movement of flaming tapers, would have been better realized in terms of geometric form, by the Knights Templar in their circular, nested ambulatories in round or octagonal temples in Florence, Bologna, Pisa, Milan, and other cities.

In the Primum Mobile the angels in their nine, individuated, sparkling and rotating rings dance in "ternaro" or triad formations (*Par.* XXVIII, 105) which lack the unity of the Trinity, each triad representing in mathematics three vectors brought together but not combined, and in music three tones of a chord composed of the root tone with its third and fifth, with or without the octave. At Chartres Chancellor Thierry had gained fame by presenting theological conceptions in such geometric formulations, reducing all geometrical and musical relations to derivations upon the unity of a geometrically conceived Trinity.

So large are the hosts of angels that their numbers are suggested by a curious numerological analogy of a sort popular in the French cathedral schools. In describing the angels as sparks thrown out by molten iron, Dante writes,

> L'incendio suo seguiva ogne scintilla;
> ed eran tante, che 'l numero loro
> più che 'l doppiar de li scacchi s'inmilla.
>
> (*Par.* XXVIII, 91–93)

> And every spark kept to its fiery ring
> and the number of their thousands to more than
> the doubling of the chessboard.

In the first triad of the angelic dance, the "cerchi primi" or "first circles" (*Par.* XXVIII, 98), swiftest and most fiery and closest to the central light, are said by Beatrice to be composed of Seraphs and Cherubs who "succeed in measure as they are sublime in vision" (*Par.* XXVIII, 102: "posson quanto a veder son soblimi"). In the circle of the sun, Dante had identified St. Francis as "all seraphic in his ardour" (*Par.* XI, 37: "tutto serafico in ardore"); St. Benedict as bathed in the splendor of "cherubica luce" or cherubic light (*Par.* XI, 39). This earlier dance in the circle of the sun by these two most angelic churchmen, and by their holiest followers and associates, is fulfilled in the whirling dance of love performed by the Seraphim and Cherubim of the inner circles. In the outer circle of the first triad, Beatrice identifies the Thrones who dance with divine aspect.

The angelic orders in this first threefold formation had been associated by Dante in the *Convivio* II, 7–11, with the Holy Ghost. Beatrice significantly remarks that true blessedness is founded on "the act of vision, not on that

FIG. 32. Charlemagne's pilgrimage to Jerusalem is commemorated at Chartres in an eastern bay of the apse. Charlemagne astride his horse strikes a Saracen during the battle of Jerusalem (lower left, second pane from bottom). The French king, returning victorious from Jerusalem, is received by the Emperor Constantine at the gates of Constantinople (center, first full pane from bottom). The Emperor presents relics of the passion to Charlemagne (lower right, second pane from bottom).

In *Paradiso* XVIII Dante views Charlemagne along with other holy warriors in a huge cross in the sphere of Mars.

which loves, which follows after" (*Par.* XXVIII, 110–111: "l'atto che vede,/ non in quel ch'ama, che poscia seconda").

Beatrice then points out in the "altro ternaro" or "second triad" the

FIG. 33. The Moses window in the Chapel of St. Peregrinus, St. Denis, reveals Old Testament events recorded both in the Bible and by pilgrimage "stations" in the Book of the World. Dante re-enacts the Exodus, and so converts his soul from sin to grace, in *Purgatorio.*

angels who primarily sing: the Dominations, Virtues, and Powers. This heavenly choir unceasingly utters "*Osanna*" with "three melodies which sound in the three orders of gladness, whereof it is three-plied" (*Par.* XXVIII, 119–120: "tre melode, che suonano in tree/ ordini di letizia onde s'interna"). Dante in the *Convivio* II had identified these orders with Wisdom and the Son.

In the final triad, Dante's lady indicates, the Principalities and Archangels "girano" or whirl; and in the outermost ring, she observes "all of Angelic

FIG. 34. In *De Administratione* Suger discussed the details of the Moses and the Exodus window situated in a northern apsidal chapel of St. Denis. Scenes of the Exodus appear in the reconstructed window: a) Moses before the burning bush at Mt. Sinai in the second circular pane from the bottom; b) Moses receiving the Law on Mt. Sinai in the second circular pane from the top.

rejoicings" (*Par.* XXVIII, 126: "tutto d'Angelici ludi"). Though the text does not clearly signify abstract meaning, Dante had noted in the *Convivio* II that this last ring represents the Father and Power.

As a prelude to Dante's final visions, the "trïunfo" or triumph of the angelic temple slowly fades as stars disappear at dawn (*Par.* XXX, 7–10); and the beauty of Beatrice appears to transcend all measure, surpassing the descriptive power first apparent in the *Vita Nuova* that had served Dante from the first day he had seen his lady "in this life" (*Par.* XXX, 29: "in questa vita"). From the commanding statements of Beatrice, Dante discovers that he is now in the Empyrean in a realm of "pure light, light intellectual full-charged with love" (*Par.* XXX, 39–40: "pura luce:/ luce intellettüal piena d' amore").

Viewing and then drinking from a luminous river that showers sparks on flowery banks—elements identified by Beatrice as "the shadowy prefaces of their reality" (*Par.* XXX, 78: "di lor vero umbriferi prefazi")—the poet at last sees that reality in a vision of the celestial city that combines astonishing amplitude, delicacy, and spiritual energy. For the river, the sparks, and the flowers seem to transform, in a marvelous fulfillment of a multiplicity of foreshadowing types of the Church Triumphant, into a glorious and subsuming garden wheel-rose, a great circle of light that sweeps over the Empyrean with a "circunferenza" (*Par.* XXX, 104) or circumference so vast that it outreaches the orbit of the sun and contains the "more than a thousand ranks" (*Par.* XXX, 113: "più di mille soglie") of those blessed in the celestial city of God. Dazzling light from the upward curvature of the lower edge of the wheel-rose above reflects the downward curvature of the upper edge of the Primum Mobile below, casting beyond the distant extremities of the celestial city a mirrored image of the outermost sphere, "as a hillside reflects itself in water at its foot" (*Par.* XXX, 109–110: "come clivo in acqua di suo imo/ si specchia"), that radiates outward through the Empyrean. This great wheel is created from a fusion of the iconographic elements in cosmic wheel windows on earth. Yet with poetic daring, Dante dramatically transforms these elements even as he relies upon them.

Earthly wheels have long been recognized as signifying a dynamic, active cosmos; and icons representing changeable Fortune were sometimes placed on the exterior of wheels such as those at Saint-Étienne, Beauvais; San Zeno, Verona; and the modified wheel of Fortune at St. Denis.[57] But unlike the rotating wheel dances and icons that appear in the *Commedia* in Eden, the circle of the sun, the Primum Mobile, and elsewhere, the great wheel rose of the Empyrean remains changeless and serene. The only movement is that of the "milizia santa" or "holy militia" (*Par.* XXXI, 2) of descending and reascending angels who, "like to a swarm of bees" (*Par.* XXXI, 7: "come schiera d'ape"), appear divinely to invert and yet correspond to natural order by carrying sweetness, not as in nature from the flower to the hive,

---

[57] See Leyerle on the San Zeno wheel-rose in "The Rose Wheel Design," 280–302. In Painton Cowen's *Rose Windows,* see plate 25 of Saint-Étienne, Beauvais (ca. 1100), and plate 26 of the modified form of a fortune-type wheel at St. Denis.

FIG. 35. The Infancy window in a northern apsidal chapel of St. Denis shows biblical episodes that were also commemorated by a special medieval chain of Holy Family pilgrimage "stations" in Egypt and the Holy Land.

but apparently from heaven down to the ranked heavenly hosts in the petals of the flower (*Par. XXXI*, 7–12). The celestial wheel-rose moreover, is a divine and virtuous white, not multi-colored as were those most intricate of wheels on earth that employed stained or painted glass to disclose in greatest iconographic detail the multitude of the blessed.

When Dante's gaze traverses within the rose the "two courts of heaven" (*Par. XXX*, 96: "ambo le corti del ciel") thronged with the personages of the Old and New Testament together with other triumphant hosts, he sees an amalgamation of images that uniquely includes the fulfilled form of the Book of God's Words that had appeared in the foreshadowing procession in Eden. In earthly temples in Italy, France, and throughout Europe, the two courts of heaven, as has been noted, were widely separated with Old Testament personages in the north transept wheel-rose and New Testament personages in the south transept wheel-rose. Dante unifies the courts in a single circle. Then too the iconographic images of Christ, the Virgin, or a divine figure, images traditionally placed at the center of the earthly wheels, are now gone from the hub of the white rose of the Empyrean. The mysterious, empty hub glows yellow. Only through Beatific Vision will Dante gaze into the whirling center of all creation.

The unfolding action of the poem, derived in part from a knowledge of wheel-rose configurations, is extraordinary. The astounded Dante is drawn by Beatrice into an exalted position: directly into the yellow hub of the rose. The wonder of the poet before the celestial city is then captured in a comparison that points back to the foreshadowing earthly experience of travelers arriving before the eternal city of Rome, a comparison that points back as well to the initial starting place of Dante's long pilgrimage as recorded in the *Vita Nuova*.

> Se i barbari, venendo da tal plaga
>   che ciascun giorno d'Elice si cuopra,
>   rotante col suo figlio ond' ella è vaga,
> veggendo Roma e l'ardüa sua opra,
>   stupefaciensi, quando Laterano
>   a le cose mortali andò di sopra;
> ïo, che al divino da l'umano,
>   a l'etterno dal tempo era venuto,
>   e di Fiorenza in popol giusto e sano,
> di che stupor dovea esser compiuto!
>
> (*Par. XXXI*, 31–40)

> If the Barbarians coming from such a region as
>   every day is spanned by Helice, wheeling
>   with her son towards whom she yearns,
> on seeing Rome and her mighty works—when
>   the Lateran transcended mortal things—
>   were stupefied;

> what then of me, who to the divine from the
>   human, to the eternal from time had passed,
>   and from Florence to a people just and sane,
> with what amazement must I have been filled!

Contemporaneous accounts reveal that during the Jubilee Pilgrimage of 1300 travelers, upon reaching Monte Mario overlooking the earthly eternal city, kissed the ground and cried, "Roma, Roma!"[58] But such exultation, though suggested by Dante's simile, is represented as a grossly inadequate measure of the transcendent stupefaction of the poet before the celestial rose. Having journeyed from Florence beyond life on a pilgrimage of Conversion, Redemption, and Transfiguration through three realms to an eternal city of the sane and just; having thus fulfilled in the *Commedia* a prefiguring earthly pilgrimage of Palmers and Romers, first mentioned in the *Vita Nuova*, from "d'Egitto/ vegna in Jerusalemme" (*Par.* XXV, 55–56) and then to Rome, Dante before the heavenly city, despite his spiritual regeneration and his acceptance of divine gifts of grace, is still like a barbarian yearning for his beloved and caught in the whirl of time. His simile deftly defines his spiritual inadequacy as a pilgrim.

The comparison also extends a remorseless criticism of the papacy of Dante's time, a criticism voiced earlier by St. Peter within physical view of Rome among the fixed stars. Although the poet's journey takes place in the Jubilee Year of 1300, the Rome to which Dante refers is the Rome of the past, the imperial city of genuine spiritual and temporal authority in which the Lateran, the palace of the papacy, transcended mortal things and was in harmony with heaven. It is this imperial and spiritual Rome that Dante through his poem announces will be reborn. Yet Dante here and in other passages shapes the foreshadowing earthly journey of his life in concord with epochal types that, while presented as sequential and "historical," are ultimately unaffected by modern empirical details of time and place that fall outside the established figural matrix. Like Petrarch who, ignoring "objective" earthly time, wrote letters to the noble dead as if they were his living companions, so Dante through the typology of his poem merges the living and dead, and past and present places and events as well, into ideal figural patterns. The poet thus criticizes the papacy of his period while alluding to a prefiguring pilgrimage to the "true" Rome in the Jubilee Year of 1300.

In an analogy focused upon himself without reference to what he sees, Dante, establishing a further relation between earthly and heavenly pilgrimage experiences, looks upward from his position beside Beatrice to the ordered personages of the rose:

---

[58] *Croniche Fiorentine,* 320. Accounts of the throngs of pilgrims appear in Caldecot Chubb, *Dante and His World,* 23–25; Lonsdale Ragg, *Dante and His Italy,* 1–39; Herbert Thurston, *The Holy Year of Jubilee,* 19–20; and Peter Armour, *The Door of Purgatory,* 155–156.

E quasi peregrin che si ricrea
   nel tempio del suo voto riguardando,
   e spera già ridir com' ello stea,
su per la viva luce passeggiando,
   menava ïo li occhi per li gradi,
   mo sù, mo giù e mo recirculando.

(Par. XXXI, 43–48)

As the pilgrim who draws fresh life in
   the temple of his vow as he gazes, and already
   hopes to tell again how it be placed,
so traversing the living light, I cast my eyes
   along the ranks, now up, now down, and now
   round circling.

The shared popular experiences that helped to give form to the medieval
Book of the World, and that provided a primary source for Dante's typology,
are indeed revealed in this concise simile. The foreshadowed earthly pilgrim
stands beside his guide in the temple of his vow, moves his eyes upward
along beams of light to ranked images and particularly those on lancet and
wheel windows, and—as the enormous international body of pilgrim texts
gives evidence—strives to remember all that he has seen, to recall the exact
placement and the relative locations of the holiest pilgrimage icons, to
relate or to write down the pattern of the icons so that persons at home
might share spiritually in the pilgrimage. But then as now a most knowledgeable guide is needed to show and to explain the most important of
the thousands of icons ranged in a pilgrimage temple. When Dante beyond
life looks again for Beatrice, he discovers that she is no longer at his side.
The mystic St. Bernard, the last guide, is now beside the poet.

Lifting his eyes to the great wheel-rose, Dante sees Beatrice within it
making a crown for herself and reflecting the eternal ray. In Chapter
XXXVIII of the *Vita Nuova*, it will be recalled, this lady was said to have
been uplifted into heaven under the banner of the Virgin Mary. Now Beatrice actually appears to the poet in the "third circle from the highest rank"
(*Par.* XXXI, 67–68: "terzo giro/ dal sommo grado") below the Virgin Mary
who is enthroned at the summit of the outermost ring. Dante writes of
how his lady smiled upon him and then, assuming the posture in which
she was last described in the earlier work, "turned her to the eternal fountain" (*Par.* XXXI, 93: "poi si tornò a l'etterna fontana").

In Chapter XL of the *Vita Nuova*, the movement of pilgrims through
Florence on their way to Rome to view "that blessed image which Jesus
Christ left to us for a figura" ("la quale Gesù Cristo lasciò a noi per esempio
della sua bellissima figura"), was seen to foreshadow the pilgrimage of
Dante's sign to Beatrice who was looking upon Godhead in heaven. The
"blessed image" or Veil of Veronica was indeed a figura of Beatific Vision;
Pardoners, as is revealed in *Piers Plowman*, and pilgrims returning from

FIG. 36. The flight of the Holy Family into Egypt is depicted in the Infancy window, second circular pane from the top.

FIG. 37. On the curved thirteenth-century archivolts on the south central porch at Chartres, and in Dante's circular temple of the angels in *Paradiso* XXVIII, the nine angelic orders appear following the classifications in Pseudo-Dionysius' *De Caelesti Hierarchia*. Below the archivolts in the tympanum, Christ Incarnate displays on side, feet, and upraised hands the Crucifixion wounds.

Rome sewed miniature figura of the veil on their garments and so carried the image throughout Christendom.[59] Francesco Petrarch, who described his own Jubilee Pilgrimage to Rome in Book II, epistle nine of his *Familiar Letters*, composed sonnet XVI about an aging man's journey in his last days to this holiest of relics at Old St. Peter's Basilica.[60]

When Dante looks from Beatrice into the countenance of his nearby guide St. Bernard, the poet at this juncture is compared to a pilgrim from Croatia or some other distant land, a pilgrim still yearning for true vision, but one who grows doubtful upon viewing the briefly shown relic of the divine image.

> Qual è colui che forse di Croazia
>   viene a veder la Veronica nostra,
>   che per l'antica fame non sen sazia,
> ma dice nel pensier, fin che si mostra:
>   "Segnor mio Iesù Cristo, Dio verace,
>   or fu sì fatta la sembianza vostra?";
> tal era io mirando la vivace
>   carità di colui che 'n questo mondo,
>   contemplando, gustò di quella pace.
>
> (Par. XXXI, 103–111)

> As is he who comes perhaps from Croatia
>   to look on our Veronica, and whose old
>   desire is not sated,
> but says in thought so long as it is shown:
>   "My Lord Jesus Christ, true God, and was
>   this, then, the fashion of your semblance?"
> such was I, gazing upon the living love of him
>   who, in this world, in contemplation tasted
>   of that peace.

The foreshadowing actions of an earthly pilgrim in an eternal city—actions distilled, intensified, and merged in the fulfilled activities of Dante before and within the celestial city—have been specifically examined in other studies. Yet whatever earthly pilgrimage experiences Dante combined and "adjusted" to create "true," fulfilled events in the world beyond, the typology of the poem suggests the foreshadowing place and action of the final vision. Dante has *in figura* moved over the pathway taken by Aeneas

---

[59] These pilgrimage practices are discussed in *The Vision of Dante*, trans. with notes by Henry Francis Carey (London, 1929), in commentary on *Par.* XXXI, 95; p. 557.

[60] The description by Francesco Petrarch of his emotional reactions, during his Jubilee Pilgrimage to Rome in 1350, appears in *Epistolae Familiares* (Venezia, 1942), Bk. 2, Letter 9. See also Petrarch's sonnet xiv in *Le Rime di Francesco Petrarca*, notes by Giosue Carducci and Severino Farrari (Firenze, 1946), 17–18, about an aged man who in his last days makes a journey to Rome to see the famed image of Christ on the Veil of Veronica.

FIG. 38. This early Wheel of Fortune without glass panes, a wheel entirely carved into the stone facade of Saint-Étienne, Beauvais (ca. 1100), is a precursor of the great stained glass rose-wheels at Chartres, Notre Dame, Rheims and other cathedrals. On the outer edge people are rendered being dragged past two dragons toward a headless monster holding a club. Wheel window designs, like the wheel icons of Dante's *Commedia*, signify the contrast between the material realms of time and change and the immaterial realm of eternity.

and St. Paul to that earthly eternal city in which sits the enthroned papal successor of St. Peter (*Inf.* II, 23–24); and in the world beyond in fulfillment of that foreshadowed journey he has arrived before the "città" or city and the "alto seggio" or high seat (*Inf.* I, 128) of the divine Emperor of the eternal heavenly realm. In his twofold pilgrimage, the poet has come to his stated destination at the "gate of St. Peter" (*Inf.* I, 134: "porta di san Pietro") before the heavenly hosts in what Beatrice has called "nostra basilica" or our basilica (*Par.* XXV, 30); and he has embodied in his otherworldly actions the prefiguring experiences of Romers on earth who view the relic of the Veil of Veronica at St. Peter's Basilica in the eternal city. Although Dante's final vision of the celestial rose is so spiritually resplendent that it is only slightly suggested by earthly types, figural contexts having their origins in the *Vita Nuova*, but greatly expanded in the *Commedia*, point

FIG. 39. The Occidental Wheel-Rose, Chartres. (a) Exterior.

FIG. 39. (b) Interior. The giant 13.36-meter wheel-rose (ca. 1216), depicting Christ at the center of the angels and the twelve Apostles, projects focused rays of afternoon sunlight down upon a huge and corresponding circular inlaid stone labyrinth on the nave floor below. At the hub of the wheel-rose, Christ shows the wounds of the Crucifixion. Immediately next to Christ, twelve small lights depict the angels and the four symbols of the Evangelists. In the larger outer circles of these same surrounding panes, the twelve Apostles appear in pairs in the lower panes. St. Peter holds a key in the circle directly to the left of Christ. The souls of the blessed are represented in the top circular panes; evil souls are shown descending in a pane at the bottom right.

88

to a continued unfolding of prefigured action in an obvious earthly setting and event: the vast interior of the Byzantine-Romanesque basilica of Old St. Peter's containing a sixth-century wheel-rose window installed under Pope Gregory III high in the Eastern facade. This is the figured earthly setting in which a Romer, at the direction of a guide, gazes upward from the basilica's holy "center" along a beam of light to heavenly iconographic forms and cosmic circles in a translucent wheel-rose illumined by the morning sunrise.

Beginning an experience of transfiguring vision, Dante raises his eyes, never to lower them to his guide again, toward the rose's vast and shimmering brightness that constantly appears to increase in luminosity "as at morn the oriental regions of the horizon overcome that where the sun declines" (*Par.* XXXI, 118–119: "come da mattina/ la parte oriental de l'orizzonte/ soverchia quella dove 'l sol declina"). His eyes move "as from a valley . . . to a mountain" (*Par.* XXXI, 121: "quasi di valle . . . a monte") past a middle region, where more than a thousand angels distinctly and individually glimmer, to the remotest far-flung reaches of the great wheel's summit. As Dante gazes, St. Bernard through his words points out the Virgin at the highest eminence, and then directs attention from "petal to petal" (*Par.* XXXII, 15: "foglia in foglia") naming a few among the biblical figures and the elect. Of the non-biblical personages visible, St. Bernard identifies only Beatrice in the upper wheel and, in a descending row in the lower wheel, St. Augustine, St. Benedict, and St. Francis.

But the great wheel disclosed by St. Bernard is peerless in being vertically bisected, in a manner foreign to traditional rose wheels on earth, by what the saint calls a "muro" or wall containing a "sacre scalee" or sacred stairs (*Par.* XXXII, 20–21).[61] The Virgin, in the central and highest place, appears in the outer ring along with St. Peter and then St. John the Evangelist on her right, Adam and then Moses on her left (*Par.* XXXII, 121–132). The steps leading down from her to the hub of the wheel are occupied by the chain of her ancestors: first Eve and then the Hebrew women, Rachel,

---

[61] Ernest Hatch Wilkins in "Dante and the Mosaics of His Bel San Giovanni," *Dante in America: The First Two Centuries,* ed. A. Bartlett Giamatti (Binghamton, 1983), 144–159, reprinted from *Speculum* 2 (1927): 1–10, draws a comparison between the image of Mary in Dante's city of the rose in *Paradiso* and the mosaics in the *tribuna* of the Florentine Baptistery showing Mary. In the *tribuna* mosaics Mary is depicted enthroned on the right outside of and facing away from a circular ceiling design depicting eight Old Testament figures, each within bell-shaped compartments. On the opposite side of the circular design, John the Baptist is similarly enthroned outside of and facing away from the central figures (See plate 3, p. 155). If as is possible Dante was influenced by the Baptistery mosaics in developing his images of Mary and the celestial rose, it still needs to be emphasized that the unique design of Dante's rose in *Paradiso* illustrates the transforming power of the poet's creative intuition. Unlike the image of Mary in the *tribuna* of the Florentine Baptistery, the Mary of the *Paradiso* is enthroned within and at the summit of the great rose; John the Baptist is directly to her right; and a wall with steps descends from her feet and contains places for both Old and New Testament figures.

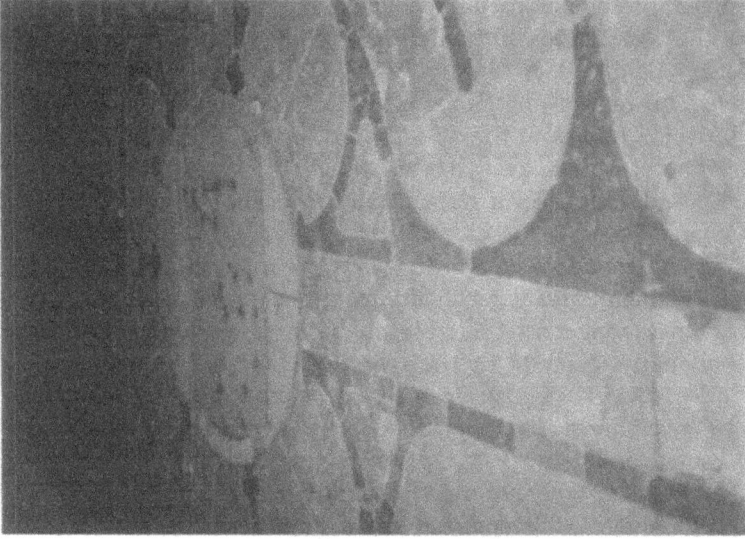

FIG. 41. The remains of fastenings for a metal medallion, no longer extant, are still visible in the central stone rosette.

FIG. 40. The 12.88-meter stone labyrinth floor at Chartres, dating from at least the thirteenth century, forms a great circle across the lower nave under the west facade wheel-rose. Medieval pilgrims are believed to have negotiated the labyrinth on their knees before moving on to the main altar. They thus acted out *in figura* an Exodus pilgrimage of conversion through the maze of this world to a central "station," a rosette signifying Jerusalem.

Sarah, Rebecca, Judith, and Ruth (*Par.* XXXII, 4–10). Dante's own lady, as an earlier reference reveals (*Inf.* II, 102), is enthroned in the third ring, outside the direct line of the Virgin's ancestors, to the right of Rachel and directly under St. Peter.

Again Dante with striking poetic originality conflates rose wheel elements and renders, in a new iconographic design strongly emphasizing female figures, the traditional rose wheel iconographic motif of the ancestry of the Virgin. In the great wheel rose of France in Chartres north (ca. 1233), for example, twelve diamond-shaped panels, circling the central figure of the Virgin at the wheel's hub, illustrate her descent from Hebrew kings in the line of David.[62] The north rose of Laon (early thirteenth century) contains at its core a stained glass representation of a woman, holding a scepter of royalty, with her body divided by a ladder with nine rungs extending from her head to her feet.[63] The rungs of the ladder possibly signify royal ancestors, the nine spheres, the nine orders of angels, or other meanings; but whatever these open iconographic symbols suggest of divinely ordained hierarchical order, they compare in a general way to the design of Dante's "sacre scalee."

The straight line of the wall bisecting Dante's heavenly wheel rose is similar also to the straight, wide vertical and horizontal tracery lines that criss-crossed the circular Tuscan wheel rose windows in cathedrals such as those at Siena (ca. thirteenth century) and the Duomo of Florence—the last under construction without the wheel-rose window in place when Dante was prior in 1300. These tracery lines, though never actually bisecting the circles, give to the balanced pattern of oblong window panels a static quality that constrasts sharply with the effect of motion conveyed by the spokes of French Gothic wheels.[64]

Like the lesser but triumphant wheel of the angelic temple that synthesizes and fulfills the circles of the physical universe and the holiest of earthly temples, the circle of the celestial city has a form that reflects elements from a range of cosmic wheels on earth, combining the petals of Northern Gothic, the wide lines of Tuscan windows, the empty hub of early Gothic, the single circle of Old and New Testament figures traditionally separated in north and south windows, and the seemingly static form of certain Italian windows. Yet through the serene and luminous immensity of the cosmic rose of Mary and of love, a rose that paradoxically fulfills even as it transcends all earthly models, Dante presents a brilliantly realized image of the eternal, Augustinian City of God ruled under the regency of Mary by the Imperial Emperor of heaven. And subsumed within the city

---

[62] Cowen, figures 6 and 7.

[63] Cowen, figure 31.

[64] See Swaan, *The Gothic Cathedral,* 289–290; plates showing the Siena window with bisecting tracery lines appear as figures 343 and 353.

is the ultimate iconographic form, depicted through named or suggested biblical personages, of the Book of God's Words.

From the moment that his new life began until the moment of his final vision of his lady within the city, Dante had been individually guided on the journey of his life by Beatrice. As a fulfilled pilgrim, Dante last looks upon his lady in the Church Triumphant as she sits, enthroned beneath St. Peter, reflecting the eternal light. The Father of the Church of Rome in turn sits at the right hand of Mary at the summit of the city of heaven.

Yet the Imperial Emperor of the celestial city is not fully manifest. The divine beam of the Emperor, though radiating down upon the city, has its source in mystical depths afar. And no iconographic image of the Emperor glows at the celestial city's yellow hub, now mysteriously occupied by Dante and St. Bernard, as it did in mortal wheels on earth. In the great circle of the celestial city, the "ancient and the modern folk" (*Par.* XXXI, 26: "gente antica e in novella") must gaze upward toward the light of Godhead emanating from what appears as the threefold brilliance of a single star. Eulogizing the light in a terza rima, Dante writes,

> Oh trina luce che 'n unica stella
> scintillando a lor vista, sì li appaga!
> guarda qua giuso a la nostra procella!
>
> (*Par.* XXXI, 28–30)

> O threefold light, which in a single star, glinting
> upon their sight doth so content them, look
> down upon our storm.

At a sign from St. Bernard, the poet of his own spiritual volition lifts his eyes to the Virgin Mary, and then follows the direction of the Virgin's gaze toward the divine illumination. With optical powers now purged and increased in virtue, the poet looks upward with ever greater depth and lucidity into the "beam of the deep light which in itself is true" (*Par.* XXXIII, 53–54: "raggio/ de l'alta luce che da sé è vera") that streams down upon him at the center of the rose. It is at this culminating moment of pilgrimage that the poet gazes upon what appears as the "semplice lume" or simple flame that is the unifying spiritual core and the ingathering, sustaining, and creatively moving infinite power underlying the "volume" or book of the entire universe. This is the flame that is the fulfillment and transcendent form of the reflected light of Beatrice's eyes, of the radiance of the sensible sun, of the angelic temple's point of spiritual light, of the threefold and yet single beam raying down upon the blessed in the rose. And when in Dante's vision the flame transfigures into what seems three rotating, fiery rings, these iconographic nested wheels fulfill and synthesize an extraordinary progression of multiple poetic images of primal light, mirrored light, movement, separate and merged color, and geometric and human form. Unlike all other wheel icons in the poem, the three luminous, whirling,

FIG. 42. The Hebrew ancestors of the Virgin, represented by personages in Dante's heavenly rose, are depicted in the north wheel-rose at Chartres (ca. 1233). Hebrew ancestors in the line of David appear in the large squares. Next to the Virgin in round panes are angels from the celestial hierarchy and, descending over her, four white doves.

Floral icons of the kind used by Dante in *Paradiso* are evident here in the window's fleurs-de-lis designs, designs having both biblical and royal signification. In *Paradiso* XXXII, the Virgin appears within a heavenly wheel-rose above a chain of Hebrew women who are her ancestors.

mirroring wheels are equal in the magnitude of their light and the speed of their rotation. "Tre colori" or three colors (*Par.* XXXIII, 117), unnamed, shimmer in and from the three wheels, the colors reflecting from wheel to wheel "like rainbow from rainbow" (*Par.* XXXIII, 118: "come ira da ira"). The light and colors of the second wheel seem mirrored in the first, and those of the third wheel, in both the first and second. Because the wheels are both sources and reflectors of light, even Dante is not entirely detached from the mirrored images he observes. For it is in the second circle that the poet finally sees, in its own color, "nostra effige" or our image (*Par.* XXXIII, 131).

Through the rational power of his creative intuition, Dante thus projects into his work a circular core icon, comparable to visual images of Godhead at the center of wheel rose windows, and yet through poetry having dimensions of suggestiveness, beyond the purely visual, that brilliantly signify

JOHN G. DEMARAY

FIG. 43. Notre Dame, Paris, north (ca. 1285, restored). The Hebrew religious background of the Virgin is a theme both of this window and of *Paradiso* XXXII. Hebrew prophets are here shown rotating about the Virgin. At the hub of this vast wheel-rose, the Christ child held by the Virgin signifies a culmination of history.

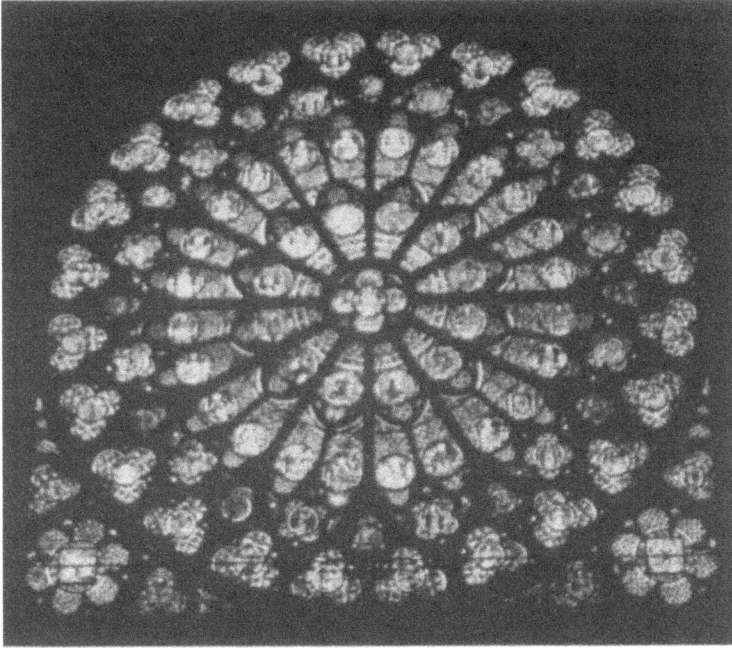

FIG. 44. Notre Dame, Paris, south (ca. 1260, reconstructed). Christ circled by the twelve Apostles, the four Evangelists and twenty-four martyrs and confessors.

Only from the main altars at the crosspoint of cathedrals could worshippers gaze upward and fully see the three great traditional wheel-roses of medieval churches: Old Testament icons in the north transept cosmic window; New Testament icons in the cosmic window of the south transept; and Revelation and heavenly city icons in the cosmic window of the nave's western facade. In *Paradiso* Dante brilliantly merges and transforms, in a single rose of heaven, identifiable elements from the three traditional windows.

the unity of all creation in the oneness of triune Godhead: the Son proceeding from the Father; the Holy Ghost from the Father and the Son; and Christ incarnate mirrored in Dante's and in all humanities' image. In its motion, undefined colors, self-perpetuating and reflecting radiance, all-subsuming quality, and human and divine iconographic design, the icon comprehensively fulfills and transcends the motionless lower wheel of the rose, embodying the Book of God's Words, in the dynamic, turning, perfect circles of the Book of Creation and of Godhead.

Dante's last mystical guide in the Empyrean, St. Bernard, in his actual historical works had avoided using extended analogies and metaphors when writing of his own beatific visions. Bernard, after first denying the possibility of such visions in his letter to the Carthusians of 1125, began first to refer to visions in composing, probably between 1129 and 1135, *De Gradibus Humilitatis*, a work of meditative steps in the anchorite-monastic tradition of John Climacus's *Scala Paradisi* and St. Bonaventure's *Itinerarim mentis in Deum.* Bernard in steps seven and twenty-one of *De Gradibus Humilitatis* writes from the assumption that man can experience vision; and in step eight, he argues at length that St. Paul had been "caught up" into the highest heaven and there gazed upon Godhead.[65] Then in his twenty-third sermon on Canticles, Bernard in 1137 made the first of many public announcements of his own mystical experiences.[66] Responding to questions about his visions, Bernard in sermon eighty-five on Canticles observes that they are beyond his own power as an adult to explain and are best revealed, through the gift of grace, in the experience of infants:

O quisquis curiosus es scire quid sit hoc, Verbo frui; para illi non aurem sed mentem. Non docet hoc lingua, sed docet gratia. Absconditur a sapientibus et prudentibus, et revelatur parvulis.[67]

O thou who art curious to know what it is to enjoy the Word, do not prepare your ear for this but your mind. The tongue does not teach this, but grace does. It is hid from the wise and prudent, and revealed unto babes.

Attaining in the context of the *Commedia* to that grace and humility of which St. Bernard wrote, Dante gives poetic expression to his beatific vision through allusions to the earliest possible remembered experience of delight and to the popular "mother arts" of clothing and architecture. He defers to the medieval scholastic conception of the fine and practical arts as knowledge for the end of making, and humbly compares himself as a poet of "primo amore" or primal love to the "careful tailor who to the cloth he has cuts the garment" (*Par.* XXXII, 140–141: "buon sartore/ che com' elli ha del panno fa la gonna"). And under the architectural influence of those earthly wheels of glass and stone that signified the immaterial realm of perfection, the physical circles of the spheres, the circle of the physical earth, and even the circle of the Garden of Eden, Dante realizes his poetic vision in an icon of rotating circles mirroring a human form. Still, in the presence of Godhead, Dante's finite human powers of speech and memory increasingly fail (*Par.* XXXIII, 106–108). And in the presence of the divine turning wheels, these two powers so diminish that Dante, like St. Bernard, can only compare the experience to that of an infant:

Omai sarà più corta mia favella,
pur a quel ch'io ricordo, che d'un fante
che bagni ancor la lingua a la mammella.

(*Par.* XXXIII, 106–108)

Now shall my speech fall farther short even of
what I can remember, than an infant's who
still bathes his tongue at the breast.

---

[65] *The Steps of Humility,* Latin text with English trans., intro. and notes by George Bosworth Burch (Cambridge, Mass., 1940), 168–169.
[66] Sermon 23 on Canticles 15 in *Opera Omnia,* vol. 1, 4th ed., ed. John Mabillon (Paris, 1839), 2803.
[67] *Opera Omnia,* 1: 3193–3194.

FIG. 45. In the south transept wheel-rose of St. Denis (ca. 1265), attributed to Pierre de Montreuil, zodiac icons of time and change form a middle ring within the circle of the cosmos. Christ, the Master of time and change in the hub representing eternity, gives a blessing encircled by the traditional twelve holy figures.

Dante in *Paradiso* is guided to eternity by points of light at the center of moving rings of holy figures sometimes arranged, as in the circle of the sun, in groups of twelve. The poet sometimes identifies the position of the rings by referring to visible signs of the zodiac.

The last analogy in all of the *Commedia* may seem disconcertingly logical to modern readers, for one of the analogical terms poses an issue in medieval geometrical theology. Dante longs to know "how the image conformed to

JOHN G. DEMARAY

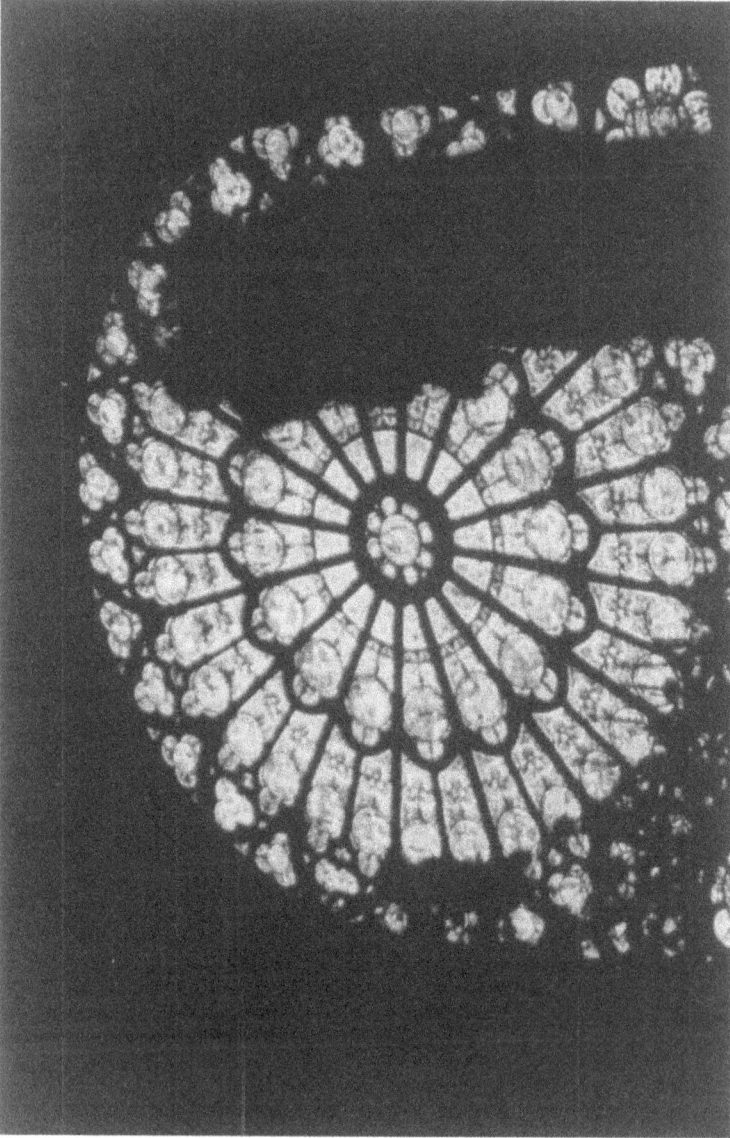

FIG. 46. Full view of the Notre Dame, Paris, north wheel-rose framed by a statue on the right. Beyond the Virgin and the surrounding Hebrew prophets at the center of this extraordinarily delicate wheel-rose, Kings and Judges appear in the second circle, high priests in the outermost circles. The window's intricate tracery, filled with approximately 700 panes and an estimated 50,000 pieces of glass, has been shown to be developed from metaphysical-geometrical, sixteen-point star-within-star designs.

In *Paradiso* XXXI Dante gazes upward at the wheel-rose of the heavenly city moving his eyes up, down, and then around in a circle.

the circle and how it has its place therein" (*Par.* XXXIII, 137–138: "come si convenne/ l'imago al cerchio, e come vi s'indova"). In seeking a solution the poet compares himself to a "geometra" or geometer who tries to square the circle and "finds not, in pondering, the principle of which he is in need" (*Par.* XXXIII, 134–135: "non ritrova,/ pensando, quel principio ond' elli indige"). Divine-human Godhead like the problem of squaring the circle, Dante notes, is logically unfathomable. Yet in focusing part of his question on how a divine-human image conforms to a circle, the poet raises, in a transcendental context, a problem exactly parallel to that actually confronted by medieval architectural masters and their apprentices in relating and placing one or more human images, formed in stained glass, within the intricate geometrical-theological tracery of the cosmic wheels on earth. Employing Trinitarian geometry of a kind made famous by Chancellor Thierry of Chartres, multiple geometrical design plans were developed and superimposed one upon the other, recent studies have shown, in constructing the final cosmic wheel outline signifying the mystery of an ordered diversity subsumed in divine oneness.

At Chartres, for example, above the labyrinth floor representing the tortuous pilgrimage route in this life to the holy city of Jerusalem, the great cosmic West Rose, showing the heavenly city of Revelation with Christ at the center surrounded by the apostles and the angels, has been analyzed as being geometrically structured from five different superimposed designs. One of these designs, Painton Cowen points out elaborating upon studies by John James, is

built up on two units measured . . . in Roman feet of 29.6 cm; one of 3 feet and another of 10 feet, which reduces to ⅔ and ⅓ to give 6⅔ and 3⅓ feet (an expansion of the number 3, and a division by 3, being a neat echo of Thierry's preoccupation with the geometric configuration of the Trinity).[68]

In calling attention to a geometrical problem relating to a wheel icon, even though this problem is logically insoluble, Dante through his analogy would have invariably brought to the mind of his contemporaries similar problems in theological-geometry that were by contrast brilliantly solved. For the "proof" of the geometry resided, not only in the magnificent tracery of the greatest earthly wheel windows, but in the flying buttresses, the vaulted roofs, the harmoniously divided nave aisles, and the balanced cruciform plans of many European "temples." In a period of widespread disease, political upheaval, and early death, these constructs of divine geometry

---

[68] Cowen, 122–123. See also John James, "Medieval Geometry," *Architectural Association Quarterly* 5, no. 2 (1973): 4–10. It should be noted also that the movement of Dante's wheels is related by John Freccero—in "The Final Image, *Paradiso* XXXIII, 144," *Dante: The Poetics of Conversion,* 248–250, reprinted from MLN, 79 (1964), 14–27—to biblical commentary by Pseudo-Dionysius, the theologian of light who influenced the builders of rose wheels. Freccero argues that the motions of Ezekiel's wheel (Ezekiel 1:16 and 10:2), as interpreted in Pseudo-Dionysius' *De caelesti hierarchia* XV, 9, are reflected in the motions of the wheels in Dante's poem.

expressed the collective aspirations of village, town, and city; for as icon-ographic constructs they both embodied the form of the universe and also served as communal centers, hospitals, religious houses, and pilgrimage sites. Dante's wheel icons in the *Commedia*, like the over-all cosmic figural design of the poem, demonstrate that the poet owed a debt to the largely unknown geometers, glaziers, stone masons, sculptors, artisans, and master builders of the cathedrals.

At the conclusion of the *Purgatorio* and the *Paradiso*, the deepest spiritual realities by degrees overwhelm certain of Dante's human powers, in accord with the stage reached in pilgrimage, even as the poet's faculties are en-lightened. Before Beatrice in the Earthly Paradise, Dante at first falls van-quished by past sin. His mind, though later illumined, still also seems spiritually "ingombra" or incumbered; and he claims to capture in words only a shadow of the living light manifest in the garden (*Purg.* XXXI, 139–145). Before the transforming icons of Godhead, the poet has been observed to suffer a nearly total failure of memory and speech. His logical reason is confounded. But having seemingly reached the outermost limits of his spiritual capacities, Dante is remarkably "smitten"; and he finally experi-ences Beatific Vision.

Unexpectedly and miraculously, Dante's mind is struck by a jolting "flash" of apprehension as the poet's intuitive reason, suddenly illumined through the gift of grace and instantaneously and effortlessly turned to-wards its end in God, gains in the frame of its human powers transfiguring mystical insight into the Divine.[69] "My mind," the poet concisely writes, "was smitten by a flash wherein its wish came to it" (*Par.* XXXIII, 140-141: "mia mente fu percossa/da un fulgore in che sua voglia venne"). Yet even as his immaterial mind is instantaneously illumined and moved, Dante experiences the loss of his lesser and now unnecessary power to receive visual images from external reality. His words are brief and dramatic: "Here power failed the lofty phantasy" (*Par.* XXXIII, 142: "A l'alta fantasia qui mancò possa").

Virgil, speaking of ordinary apprehension in which the image-receiving power is retained, had explained this movement of the mind to Dante in *Purgatorio*.

> Vostra apprensiva da esser verace
>   tragge intenzione, e dentro a voi la spiega,
>   sì che l'animo ad essa volger face;

[69] In a recent elaboration of medieval mystical writings and neo-scholastic philosophic theory, Jacques Maritain in *Man's Approach to God* (Latrobe, 1960) defines those constituants traditionally associated with Beatific Vision of a kind depicted by Dante: a "primary intuitive flash" of apprehension (pp. 13–15), "spiritual dynamism" involving a movement of the soul (pp. 20–21), and a moment of vision when "all particular representations have vanished away. . . . The God of faith is experienced by his reverberation, His implanting in love" (p. 41). Maritain in *Creative Intuition in Art and Poetry* (New York, 1953) applies a restatement of medieval conceptions of rational intuitive apprehension to comments on Dante's *Commedia*

e se, rivolto, inver' di lei si piega,
  quel piegare è amor, quell è natura
  che per piacer di novo in voi si lega.
Poi, come 'l foco movesi in altura
  per la sua forma ch' è nata a salire
  là dove più in sua matera dura,
così l'animo preso entra in disire,
  ch'è moto spiritale, e mai non posa
  fin che la cosa amata il fa gioire.

(XVIII, 22–33)

Your faculty of apprehension draws an
  image from a real existence and displays
  it within you, so that it makes the mind turn toward it
And if, being turned, the mind inclines toward it,
  that inclination is love; that inclination is nature,
  which is bound in you anew in pleasure.
Then, even as fire moves upward by reason of
  its form, whose nature is to ascend to where
  it lasts longest in its matter
So the enamoured mind falls captive to desire,
  which is a spiritual movement, and never rests
  until the object of its love make it rejoice.

While the perfection of Godhead overpowers Dante's lower faculties, the poem is not radically undermined in its epistemology or aesthetically "fragmented" in any essential way by the inescapable human failures of its narrator. Dante never presents himself, in the manner of some Reformation and many modern artists, as composing his work from his own autonomous subjectivity. His rich subjectivity is self-evident, but it is a subjectivity depicted in medieval fashion as divinely guided from without, in symmetry with his individual choice and desire, into wider conformity with the external cosmos and "true" universal history. Through divine external intervention as well as through interior volition, Dante's faltering and limited human subjectivity repeatedly subsumes initial fragmentary impressions and apprehensions in ever more virtuous unifying experiences and images. Dante's first experiences, even during Beatific Vision, are constantly being transcended. The complete range of the poet's always changing human perceptions and apprehensions reside in the language of the poem, language replete with echoes of the past and prefigurations of the future.

(pp. 370–373, and throughout). Investigations of late medieval and Renaissance views of intuitive rational apprehension can be found in Demaray, "The Inward Vision" in *Milton's Theatrical Epic: The Invention and Design of Paradise Lost* (Cambridge, Mass. and London, 1980), 1–15; and in the text and notes of Lee A. Jacobus, *Sudden Apprehension* (The Hague and Paris, 1976).

JOHN G. DEMARAY

FIG. 47. Like the luminous wheels of Dante's Beatific Vision in *Paradiso* XXXIII, this "first" true wheel-rose (ca. 1144) in the western facade of St. Denis has been associated with the biblical wheel of Ezekiel. Four enclosing zodiac signs, signifying the four Evangelists, serve as figural fulfillments of the four creatures seen by Ezekiel in the fiery wheel. This dynamic wheel-rose, placed to radiate beams of sunlight through the church dedicated to Pseudo-Dionysius, is believed to be the first to be filled with stained glass.

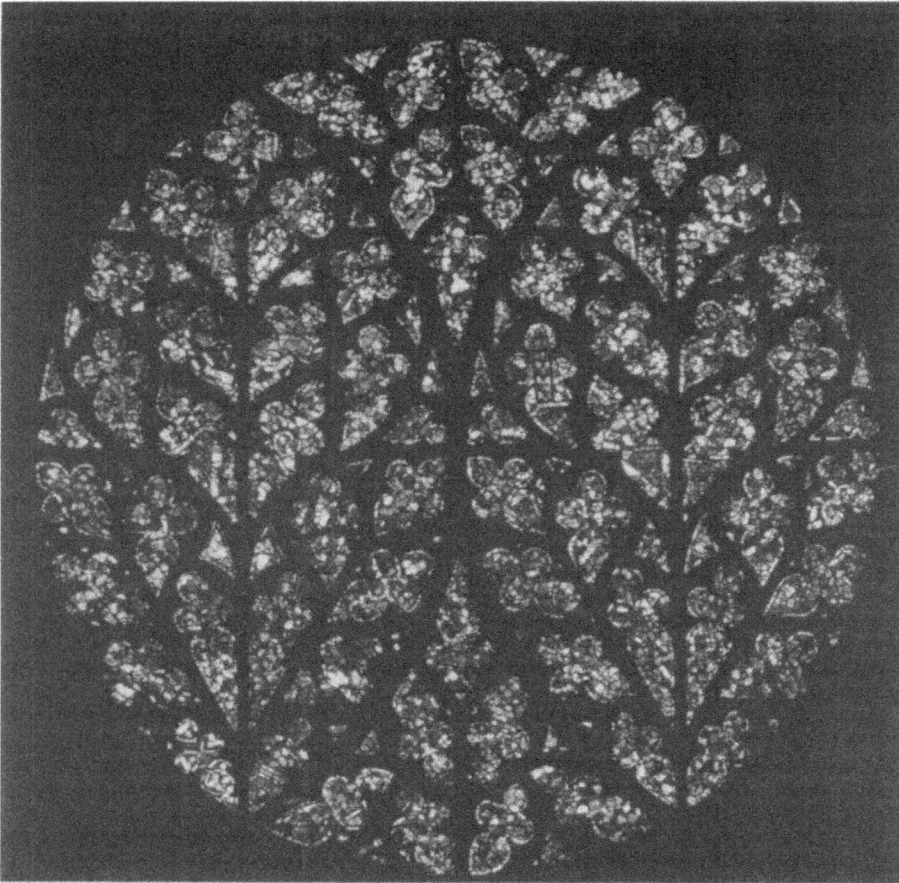

FIG. 48. The south transept wheel-rose of Lincoln cathedral (ca. 1210, restored), in the manner of Dante's final icons of Godhead in *Paradiso* XXXIII, "ingathers" the leaves of created being within the all-encompassing volume of a perfect, circular cosmos. The recurring living leaves of the cosmic volume, in *vesica piscis* form, merge in a luminous interplay of large leaf designs, intermediate leaf designs, and thousands of tiny leaf-shaped glass fragments.

The window, referred to in a poem of the thirteenth century as one of the two "oculi" of the church, was constructed under Bishop of Lincoln Robert Grosseteste, the formulator of scientific-metaphysical optical theories and the teacher of Roger Bacon.

It is from the divinely directed universal nature of the poet's spiritually fulfilling and deeply experienced actions, even more than from the poet's individualized and slow but finally enlightened human understanding of what transpires, that Dante is joined *in figura*—and by inference the reader and all persons might be as well—to the underlying form and movement of external reality. And it is primarily through re-enactment of the Exodus, the Redemption, and the Transfiguration that the poem is "grounded," not by modern "referents," but by medieval historical, typological bonds to "true" historical events recorded in Books of God represented as accessible to the connatural knowledge of Dante and his readers. The Bible, initially

signified in the procession in the Earthly Paradise and then in the fulfilled
personages of the heavenly rose, is accordingly present at those first and
last wondrous moments when Dante gazes into the eyes of his lady. The
"volume" of the Cosmos, progressively unveiled to Dante during his twofold journey and then largely synthesized and reflected from Beatrice's
eyes at the edge of the stellar sphere, is brilliantly and completely "ingathered" in the very icons of Godhead to which the poet, following the
gaze of his lady, lifts his own eyes in the Empyrean.

Though in the light of Infinite Being the leaves of the Book of the World,
the spheres, and the immaterial cosmos appear as "si squaderna" or scattered (*Par.* XXXIII, 87), the poem itself divulges, from a human point of
view, the ordered twofold, universal biblical-pilgrimage path through lower
mazes to holy centers in the ascending hierarchy of creation. And though
the words of scripture are said to be sometimes thrust aside or behind (*Par.*
XXIX, 88–89); and though these words, as Beatrice declares, "condescende"
or condescend to man "assigning foot and hand to God with other meaning"
(*Par.* IV, 44–45: "e piedi a mano/ attribuisce a Dio e altro intende"), still
these words are represented as pointing to "true" universal history, re-
enacted by Dante, in accord with the reader's human capacity objectively
to understand. "Were not the Scripture over you," the Divine Eagle of
Justice announces to Dante in the sphere of Jupiter, "there were marvelous
ground for questioning" (*Par.* XIX, 83–84: "se la Scrittura sovra voi non
fosse,/ da dubitar sarebbe a maraviglia").

Having looked into the luminous source of creation, Dante, impelled by
the external power of divine love in harmony with his own desire and will,
is moved for the last time. His movement is profoundly spiritual. It is a
transcendent interior imitation of the circular wheeling of the sparkling
angels, first manifested "inverted" in Beatrice's eyes, about that point of
divine brightness at the center of the immaterial angelic temple bordering
the stars. It is the penultimate interior re-enactment of the spiritual and
physical circular whirling of the scintillating theologians about the sun, of
the steady rotation of the planets and spheres in the temple of the physical
universe, of even the lowly foreshadowing processional movements of
figured terrestrial celebrants in the most sacred pilgrimage temples of this
world.

Dante is at last turned in concord with the universe.

> ma già volgeva il mio disio e 'l *velle*,
> sì come rota ch'igualmente è mossa,
> l'amor che move il sole e l'altre stelle.

> (*Par.* XXXIII, 143–145)

> But already my desire and will were revolved—
> even as a wheel that moves equally—by the
> Love that moves the sun and the other stars.

Sancti Sepulcri, church of, Florence, 24n
Sandoli, Fr. Sabino de, 13n; on first Franciscan "house" in Jerusalem, 29n
San Giovanni al Sepolcro, church of, Brindisi, 20
San Stefano, Bologna, 8n
Santa Croce, church of, Gerusalemme, Rome: "Imago pietatis" mosaic in, 37n; mosaics of Transfiguration in, 36n
Santarcangeli, Paolo, 21n, 23n
Santa Stefano Rotondo, Rome, 24
San Zeno, basilica of, Verona: and Dante's rose, 4; wheel of Fortune at, 79
Sarah: in celestial rose, 91
Satan: hair of, and Dante, 16; tomb of, 7, 8, 67
Scala Paradisi (John Climacus), 28, 28n, 31, 95
Schermerhorn, Elizabeth Wheeler, 9n
Schnapp, Jeffrey T., 36n
Scripture: signified in types, 3
Sens: churches of, 21n; town of, 20
Sepulchre, Holy. See Holy Sepulchre
Seraphim: and dancing, 75
Seraphs: as dancers, 75
Shapiro, Marianne: on figurism in Vita Nuova, 14n
Siena, cathedral of: rose window of, 91
Sigh, of Dante: described in sonnet, 32
Silvia of Aquitania, Saint (Egeria): describes procession in Jerusalem, 69n; as pilgrim, 56
Simson, Otto von, 20n; on cathedral and Cosmos, 1–2n; on navel of world, 20
Sinai, 16n
Sinai, Mount, 26, 27; in directional diagram, 23n; and gate of confession, 17; international pilgrims on, 27n; and Mount La Verna, 28–29; new geographic position of, 18–19; and pilgrimage steps, 31; steps to God, 28
Singleton, Charles S., 3, 6, 17n; on allegorical interpretation, 41n; his Exodus interpretation, 16n–17n; on theological allegory, 43n
Sion, Mount, 69; Holy City on, 43; Old Temple on, 67, 69
Skobucha, Heinz, 26n
Solomon's Temple, 25; rock of the altar of, 70; size of, 2
Sondoli, Sabino de, 69n
Song: as motif in architectural iconography, 73; as part of circular movements, 72, 75
Sorolli, Gian Roberto: on allegorical interpretation, 42n
Speculum: Dante's use of the word, 64
Speech: of Dante, lost before Godhead, 99, 100
SS. Cosma and Damiano, chapel of, Mt. Sinai, 26

SS. Cosma and Damiano, church of, Rome, 8n, 26
Stambler, Bernard, 36n
Stars: Dante ends each canticle with word for, 45; as guiding lights, 45; nymphs as, 45; realm of, 37–38; and the Virgin Mary, 43
Stephanos, Saint: at Gate of Confession, Mt. Sinai, 28n
Steps of Humility, The, 96n
Stigmata: and St. Francis, 27
Stigmata Chapel, on Mount La Verna, 29, 29n
Subjectivity: of Dante, in Commedia, 101
Suger, Abbot, 22, 64, 65; on chorus processions, 71–72, 75; statements about pilgrims, 20
Sumption, Jonathan, 13n
Sun: of the angels, 67; as a type for the Human-Divine Christ, 42–43; as guide to eternal vision, 45; icons of, 67
Swaan, Wim, 2n, 91n

Tabor, Mount, 18; and Mount La Verna, 28–29
T-and-O maps: of altar icons, 64; form of, 18–19; in mosaic floor at Turin, 21n
Taylor, H. O., 4
Terrasse, Charles, 2n
Theodosius I, Emperor, 25
Thierry, Chancellor, 75, 99
Thurston, Fr. Herbert, 17n, 25n, 82n
Tiber River: in Paradiso, 29
Tikken, John J., 28n
Timaeus (Plato), 2, 42n; as architectural guide, 2
Topographia Christiana, 18
Transept, church: rose wheels in, 24; windows at Lincoln Cathedral, 63
Transfiguration, 13, 18, 27; Apostles of, 18, 45; of a tree, in prefiguration of, 17; as a type, 3; and Dante, 32, 45; figured in Rome, 43; mosaics, in Rome, Ravenna, and Mt. Sinai, 26–27; re-enactment of, grounded in poem, 103; topology of, 36n
Tree of life, 69; cross made from, 70
Trinity, 42; conceived geometrically, 75; hosts of the Second Person of, 45
Troy, 23n; signified in labyrinth floors, 21
Tucker, Fr. Dunstan: and Easter Liturgy, 13n, 17n
Tuscany, 28; Mount La Verna in, 28
Typology: back-references of, 13, 16–18, 40, 40–41n, 54, 66, 67; back-references of, and Dante's autobiography, 40n; and Church Fathers, 3; of Commedia and pilgrimage churches, 20; corresponding forms, 9–19; Dante's construction of, in Commedia, 14, 82; Dante's Egypt-Jerusalem journey as, 51–54; developed progressively in Commedia, 67; forward references, 16–18, 66,